GOODBYE MISTER FIFTEEN

GOODBYE MISTER FIFTEEN

A MEMOIR

ROGER ENGLE

EDITED BY STEPHANIE ENGLE

GIRLS ON PRESS
MARTINSBURG, WV

GIRLS ON PRESS

the publishing imprint of STEPHANIE ENGLE DESIGN OFFICE

Post Office Box 6154
Martinsburg, WV 25402

WWW.GIRLSONPRESS.COM

FIRST EDITION PUBLISHED 2015.
Printed in the United States of America

19 18 17 16 15   1 2 3 4 5
ISBN: 978-0-9857134-1-6

LIBRARY OF CONGRESS CONTROL NUMBER: 2015947473

This book is printed on acid-free paper.

CONTENTS

INTRODUCTION

THE FIRST FOURTEEN YEARS OF MY CHILDHOOD had been an innocent time filled with days of fun and youthful adventures. I was a tall and awkward kid just trying to fit in and adapt to the world around me — a world that was about to change.

Up until now my world had consisted of routines. Each season brought its specific chores and expectations. Until 1962 I hadn't given much thought to world politics, but a showdown with Russia changed that. Anything related to Russia, the Island of Cuba, or outer space was dominating the news and filtering into daily life. Neighbors were constructing fallout shelters and an uneasiness seemed to descend on our little town. The United States averted war, but life would never be quite the same.

1963 arrived and everyone hoped it would be calmer. I was about to turn fifteen as West Virginia was about to celebrate its centennial. Winter began releasing its hold, and family discussions turned toward the next growing season. This included preparing for the arrival of several hundred baby chicks. We would be very busy.

The reestablished, comfortable, and routine pattern of life was suddenly broken, however, by the untimely and tragic death of Patsy Cline. She was the only "star" I knew, and the only one to have visited my home on numerous occasions. The fragile balance of life and the impermanence of things that had appeared solid once again shook the foundation of my childhood, ushering in a time of growth.

June brought with it an abundance of activity around the state as West Virginia celebrated its centennial. As a member of the high school band, I participated in a parade in nearby Martinsburg. Convening with students outside the normal school year in preparation for a civic activity was a new thing, and made me feel like I was growing up.

Summer continued to confirm that I was on the road to adulthood when my parents allowed me to purchase a car. I was only fifteen and for fifty dollars I became the proud owner of a 1949 Studebaker. With neither license nor insurance, I was instructed by my parents — rather vaguely, I might add — not to drive it "too far." My days were spent mastering the three-speed manual transmission and driving around town.

School began in September and I enjoyed everything it offered, and settled into its familiar rhythm. However, on Friday, November 22, at about one-thirty in the afternoon, the world I knew was turned upside down. It was announced that President Kennedy had been shot. Shortly thereafter, we learned that he was pronounced dead. The days that followed found my family glued to the black-and-white television, watching the news continuously. On Sunday, I watched as the president's accused killer, Lee Harvey Oswald, was shot by Jack Ruby on live television. There was no delay in the broadcast at that time.

My family returned to normalcy after immersion in the coverage of a national tragedy by shifting our focus to the upcoming holiday season. We looked forward to 1964, and prayed it would be calmer. I eagerly awaited April's arrival because I would be turning sixteen.

Before the age of sixteen, the town of Hedgesville and surrounding area had been my world. It had offered adventures and would continue to do so, but things changed on my sixteenth birthday. I had arrived at that "magic" age and could now drive. My world was expanding and the possibilities seemed endless. I started looking beyond the boundaries that once existed.

My last two years of high school were now ahead of me with all they had to offer. They would be filled with fun, excitement, and opportunity. I didn't let the academic portion of my life keep me from what some call, "the best time of their lives." School was the hub and catapult for things to come, and many adventures would originate there.

As I was getting older, what was expected of me was changing. Teachers, as well as my parents, seemed to treat me more like an adult despite the fact that I engaged in activities that appeared to prove them wrong. I was developing an internal mechanism to monitor my actions. I was realizing how my choices were affecting me and truly impacting others. Don't get me wrong — stupid things were still being done — but I now more fully understood their consequences. Each day was filled with excitement and I tried to put a positive spin on everything. How could I not be happy? I was a teenager with a car and a guitar.

There was, however, a serious element to these times. World events were once again filtering into my once simple and protected life. I was becoming familiar with places in the world I had never heard of before. Television was now bringing images into our home that no family member had ever seen. These events were becoming a part of our collective unconscious, but didn't dominate our daily lives. They would, however, soon gain greater influence.

The following stories begin when I turned sixteen. They cover both high school and college. Some are humorous and others not so much. I can't imagine my life being any other way. We only get one life and I don't think I would have changed it at all. As you read this book I hope you can sense the changes I was experiencing. It was a wonderful time and Hedgesville was a wonderful place to experience both my childhood and my youth. I wasn't experiencing it all in a vacuum though, and whether or not I resisted, the long arms of the world were pulling at me.

In one of my favorite old movies, a little girl tells her brother that she doesn't want to grow up. The brother shares a story about a boy who has a small yellow duckling he wishes would never grow up, so he squeezes it every time he thinks it is growing. Likewise, the sister is told to squeeze herself tightly when she feels herself growing, in order to remain small. The duck is squeezed to the point it dies, and the sister eventually grows up.

You can't prevent time's persistent advance, and although you can't feel the growth that is happening within you, it happens nevertheless. Hedgesville didn't squeeze me but rather nourished me and provided what I needed to face the unfolding future. I was embarking on another set of adventures on the road to adulthood. Sit back and enjoy the ride with me.

PART ONE

THE OPEN ROAD

Turning Sixteen

AS A CHILD, EVERY BIRTHDAY WAS EXCITING. THE anticipation of a gift, a special meal, or even a party made for a wonderful time. No birthday up to this point was looked forward to more than number sixteen and what it offered — the gift of mobility.

For a guy in 1964, a car was everything. With it came endless possibilities. The size of your childhood world exploded. No longer were you dependent on your feet, your bicycle, or parental assistance to go places.

How does this rapid transformation occur? In my case it began at age fifteen with fifty dollars and the purchase of a 1949 Studebaker from my Uncle Fred. I had acquired a car, but I had neither a driver's license nor insurance. My parents took these circumstances into consideration, and decided only to allow me to drive in the alleys and back roads around Hedgesville. This small playing field provided ample opportunity for mastering the stick shift. Third gear was rarely reached in the alleys, but was certainly utilized on unauthorized trips to Martinsburg.

Getting a driver's license meant you needed "The Book." This was the Department of Motor Vehicles paperback containing everything you needed to know in order to pass the written test and receive your learner's permit. I don't recall how I got my book, but I had one along with many of my classmates. We studied the words right off of the pages. I knew the content so well, in fact, that I could almost quote the page number when asked a specific question.

Shortly after turning sixteen I went to the DMV, escorted by my parents, to take the written test. This was a unique experience in and of itself due to the location. The office was part of the West Virginia State Police barracks located along Route 11, in Pikeside. It wasn't a formal structure but rather a two-story, white house. Hopeful candidates walked in the side porch entrance and nervously sat down, waiting for their names to be called.

The test was a breeze because I knew every rule and regulation in the book, whether I intended to obey any of them or not. With permit in hand we returned home. I was supposed to have a licensed driver in the vehicle with me as I practiced driving. Although I thought I was ready to take and pass the driving test the same day as passing the written test, my parents thought differently. They also had to decide which of our family vehicles to offer up as a sacrifice for my hands-on education.

At the time we had a 1959 Chevrolet station wagon and a 1955 Chevy truck. It was decided that the 1949 Studebaker would *not* be used to hone my driving skills. That left the wagon, which happened to be comparable in size to one of the largest family cars on the highway — the 1959 Cadillac.

I begged my parents relentlessly for practice time behind the wheel of our land yacht. Even though I thought I knew everything, I made my share of mistakes, the first of which was underestimating the enormous size of the car. I soon gained an appreciation of the vehicle's mass out on the highway and especially on curvy roads, which were mostly what we had. I recall my mother allowing me to drive a friend to one of our favorite fishing spots. She sat quietly as I navigated the vehicle to the stream. The wagon had an automatic transmission. When I came to a rolling stop, I thought I was in the Studebaker and proceeded to jam the shifter into park with the car still slowly moving forward. I had even depressed the imaginary clutch. That never happened again.

When my parents thought I had practiced enough, we returned to the DMV for the road test. Same white house. Same waiting room. This time, however, there was a little something different: those in front of me were being asked to read an eye chart before taking the practical exam. Being able to see is certainly a factor when driving, but I quickly learned that if you wore glasses, a restriction would be placed on your license stating the obvious: you wore glasses. I wore glasses and couldn't see to drive without them, but I certainly didn't want any restrictions on my license, even though I had no idea what limitations might be imposed.

I avoided this potential all together by memorizing the eye chart down to the line that would give me 20/20 vision. When my turn came, I put my glasses into my pocket, moved to the designated spot, and waited until I was asked to read the smallest line I could see. Amazingly, I easily demonstrated the visual acuity possible with 20/20 vision! If I had been asked to read any part of that chart from the giant E downward, without having first memorized it and without my glasses, I would have failed. In fact, even seeing the chart on the wall was a challenge. Having overcome this obstacle I was now sent outside to wait for the officer who would administer the practical exam. Since he had been outside all along, he had no idea about what had just happened with the eye chart, so on went my glasses. I had to wear them, otherwise I could not have found the highway.

I sat behind the wheel of the '59 wagon and was asked to show my knowledge of where everything was located on the car. It didn't take long because all the car had were lights, turn signals, and a horn. Next came the parking test. If you couldn't parallel park, you couldn't proceed to the highway. Many people feared this task. For me it was no problem. I had parallel parked the Studebaker hundreds of times and our station wagon was just bigger.

With this task successfully completed, I drove out onto Route 11 — the main north-south route in the county, and a very busy road. I remember not being afraid of what I was doing, and feeling confident I could drive on any highway. My concern was doing every little thing correctly. I had to remember not to stop or accelerate too fast, to use the turn signals — a habit I failed to develop during my time in the Studebaker — and try not to do something stupid.

The road test commenced as follows: enter the highway,

head south to the church; turn left, then go a short distance down the road; turn around, and re-trace the path back to the barracks; and park and wait for the officer to comment. After hearing him say I had passed, and receiving the appropriately signed document, I returned home.

Pleased as punch with my driver's license, I was introduced to the world of automobile insurance and the realization that I had to have money to pay for my newly found freedom. A phone call to the insurance company and a check from my meager bank account meant I was "road-worthy." A funny thing is, I remember my first solo trip in the '59 Chevy wagon. It was neither a date nor going to an exciting event, but rather a trip to a nearby farm to collect plants for a school project. I collected Solomon's Seal, and couldn't have been happier doing so.

I don't know if a driver's license means as much to a sixteen-year-old boy today as it meant to me in 1964. It was my "Ticket to Ride," even though the Beatles probably had something much different in mind when they titled their song. I was now free to find jobs wherever I could, and seek out the ladies. Turning sixteen pulled open the curtain and revealed many wonders beyond Hedgesville. It meant responsibility and a necessary degree of maturity.

It also meant that the '49 Studebaker and I would soon part company. It just wasn't cool enough anymore. In retrospect, however, it would be absolutely cool to have both my '49 Studebaker and my sixteenth birthday back again.

DON'T HIT THE STUDEBAKER

I T'S AMAZING HOW QUICKLY THINGS CAN CHANGE. In just one second, unbridled joy can turn into worry and even fear. This story didn't reach the point of fear, but it certainly took the polish off of a shiny moment.

Shortly after getting my driver's license, my parents allowed me to use the Chevy wagon to take some friends to the bowling alley in Pikeside, about fifteen miles away. I can't remember who was in the car, but someone needed us to make a stop along the way at the Drug Fair store in Martinsburg. I pulled into the lot, parked the car, and waited for them to return from the store.

I had parked next to a 1963 Studebaker, and both cars were facing in the same direction. Being a Studebaker-man myself, I was familiar with that car. When we were ready to leave, I started the car and slowly backed out of my parking space. I carefully guided the Chevy around the rear of the Studebaker at a snail's pace, trying to do everything correctly. Unfortunately, I made the turn a bit too sharp and the passenger-side front bumper of my car tapped the driver's-side rear bumper of the Studebaker. At the speed I was going, this should have been a "nothing" event — just a very slight tap with no damage to show for it. This was true for the Chevy, but not so for the Studebaker. I watched in total dismay as both the back and front bumpers fell off, along with assorted lights and mirrors. It looked like a chop shop had opened up in the Drug Fair parking lot!

After getting out and surveying the damages came the decision of what to do next. There had been no thud or crashing sound, just pieces of somebody's car falling onto the asphalt parking lot. I could just drive away and no one would be the wiser. That thought did cross my mind, but was quickly dismissed as my developing moral compass inconveniently emerged.

I parked the Chevy and went into the office in Drug Fair. I asked the clerk if they knew who owned the Studebaker. The owner was discovered and information was exchanged. No police were called in. I left the store and returned to my passengers and the Chevy, which had suffered absolutely no damage.

Now came the decision of continuing our trip to the bowling alley, or calling it a day. I returned to the store and used their phone to call home. I explained to my parents what had happened. They didn't seem to be too worried, so we continued our trip to the bowling alley as if nothing had happened.

A wrinkle in this story is that Studebaker Corporation had moved its operations from the United States to Canada, and parts were getting more difficult to obtain. This fact made the cost of the repairs higher for me, and lengthened the time it took to get those parts to the owner.

What I will never understand is how so much damage could have happened with just a little bump. The 1963 Studebaker I hit appeared to be built like a house of cards and literally collapsed upon contact. The 1949 Studebaker I had sitting at home was, on the other hand, built like a tank. If you remember the television show *Candid Camera*, this incident could have been set up and filmed just for it. Perhaps the car was a "plant" just waiting to be bumped and the victim's response recorded. Maybe the owner had placed the car there and rigged it, hoping something like this would happen to enable him to get his car repairs done for free. Unfortunately, Candid Camera's host, Allen Funt, never appeared, and I couldn't prove that the owner had any such plans. All I can do is sum up this story in four words — don't hit the Studebaker.

How to Blow
An Engine in a Day

THIS WAS NOT MY FIRST CAR BUT RATHER THE first car I owned and could legally drive. I bought it in the summer of 1964 for a couple hundred dollars from someone who would later become my brother-in-law — but that's another story.

It was a 1954 Ford and had a six-cylinder engine, a three-speed transmission, and no paint — just gray primer. The overall appearance of the car was clunky. The tires were, to say the least, bald. As described in the movie *A Christmas Story,* they were tires only in the sense that they were round and had once been made of rubber. Whitewall tires cost too much so I had port-a-walls. They were basically white rings attached to the rims and held in place by the inflated tire. They looked the part.

I purchased the car on a Saturday morning and couldn't wait to drive it home. To me, the Ford seemed just like a

Cadillac. That afternoon a friend and I took the car for a ride out past North Mountain. We headed toward Little Georgetown where there was a long, straight stretch of highway perfectly suited for testing my new car's speed and capabilities.

Wheels spun as we took off in first gear. Next I shifted into second gear, gave it some gas, dropped into third gear, and pressed the pedal to the floor. It just didn't seem to be going as fast as I had imagined it would go, so I dropped it back into second gear. This was a huge mistake. I don't know how many RPMs we were going, but it was enough to blow the engine. It shot a rod — or *rods* perhaps — and started throwing oil everywhere. The engine was gone the same day the car had come into my possession.

As we weren't too far from home, we made our way along Route 901, the car chugging and sputtering. Once we reached the high school it was a downhill drift to the Pure gas station where I was working part-time. This engine wasn't going to be rebuilt but rather replaced. Staley's in Harpers Ferry was my junkyard of choice. I could get an engine for under a hundred dollars and in a few hours have the car ready to go again. I got rather good at this as I did it more than once. On one occasion Nelson, who worked at the garage, decided he would help me by taking the distributor from the old engine and putting it into the newer one, thinking the old one was in better shape. This might have been so, but the problem was, the shaft was shorter on the old one. It dropped into place and tightened down correctly but the gears on the bottom of the shaft never engaged with the engine. This resulted in the engine running perfectly, but no oil being pumped into it. The engine locked up within minutes and was ruined. Don't always accept free help.

THE BIG BANG

I HAD THE 1954 FORD FOR SEVERAL YEARS AND HAD some interesting adventures. I did one thing that wasn't dangerous, but rather just stupid. While coming home from high school, which again was atop a hill, I turned the switch off for a few seconds, keeping the car in gear, and moving forward. The fuel pump was mechanical and continued to pump gas into the engine which, in turn, passed unburned into the muffler. After a few seconds I turned the switch back on and the ignition caused the unburned gas to explode with a loud bang.

On another occasion I decided to try this again, but this time I kept the switch turned off much longer and actually pumped the gas pedal to circulate more fuel into the muffler. I don't know how much gas was available but when I turned the switch back on there was a *real* explosion. It blew the muffler apart and some of the exhaust pipe was now dragging on the road. This destruction ironically happened at about the same spot on the road where years ago I had attempted to jump a dog with my bicycle, and lost my brand new wristwatch.

Not only was the explosion loud, but now there was no working exhaust on the six-banger. Not wanting to get in trouble with my parents, I crept up an alley and again drifted toward the garage. With the help of clamps and wire I got some of the exhaust reattached. It was far from perfect but better than nothing. I never did replace it, but in the days ahead wrapped more wire, added some muffler patch, and kept tightening the clamps in an attempt to keep the car in commission.

Afterschool Physics Lesson

H AVING A DRIVER'S LICENSE AND CAR SUDDENLY made it necessary to drive the short distance to school that for years I had walked. One winter a bad ice storm came through town during the school day. We rarely had an early dismissal, and this day was no exception. The roads were in terrible shape when school dismissed. Remember, every direction from the high school was downhill. I should have just left the car in the parking lot and slid home on foot, but I didn't. It mattered not to me that there was little-to-no tread on my tires. Unless you had chains on your tires, there was no control on ice anyway.

After scraping a hole in the ice on the windshield, I started the car and headed home. I quickly discovered that the brakes were no match for the combination of ice, gravity, and momentum. I kept trying to steer, but the steering wheel was of little value. I could make the front wheels turn but the car wouldn't follow my lead.

With a fenced field on one side of the road and a wooded area on the other, there was really nowhere to go and nothing to do but ride it out. What kept me from completely turning around I will never know, but I traveled sideways for quite some time. When this happened, I just let go of the steering wheel, as it was rendered useless by the ice.

This was a steep hill, and a heavy car on ice only picks up more speed. Fortunately at the bottom of the hill there was a straight and level stretch before the road intersected with Route 9. It was long enough for me to regain control of the car, straighten my path, and gently apply the brakes to come to a complete stop. When the car finally stopped moving, I collected my thoughts and decided to try and get it home. Route 9 had been cindered and provided some traction. Once home I could breathe easier.

Everyone knows that you can't drive on ice — that is, everyone except a sixteen year old with a 3000-pound, gray-colored sled with treadless tires and little common sense. It was a teachable moment.

∞

FORD SCORES A TOUCHDOWN

THESE DAYS YOU HAVE TO NAVIGATE A MAZE of fencing just to access the track around most high school football fields. There is usually an additional fence surrounding the field, and the field itself is often made of artificial turf. All of these conditions make attempting the following stunt impossible today, but in my youth we had unfettered access to our football field.

In one of our moments of deep thought, several of us decided it would be cool to see how fast a car could go in a hundred yards. The high school football field seemed the perfect proving ground, as it was clearly a hundred yards long. I decided the '54 Ford would serve as our test vehicle. We drove down the off-limits dirt access road and I stopped at the south end of the field, just under the goal post.

We were not timing the event, but rather just checking the maximum speed. We decided to try a test run first from south to north. The north goal post marked the end of our football field and the beginning of our baseball field. The test run took place without incident.

Now came the actual test, north to south. The engine was gunned and infield dirt flew. Second gear was hit about midfield. We gained speed, heading to the south goal post. As it quickly grew closer, I was presented with an urgent dilemma: when to let off of the gas and apply the brakes. Just a few yards of field extended beyond the south goal post, followed abruptly by a dirt bank.

It became evident I had to hit the brakes immediately, or risk hitting the dirt bank. I smashed the brake pedal to the floor and we began a sideways slide toward the end zone. We slid past the goal post and stopped just shy of the dirt bank. Touchdown!

There were several problems with our test, however: in our excitement we failed to look at the speedometer to check our maximum speed; and behind us were deep ruts in the football field, beginning at about the twenty-yard line and extending into the end zone. We left the scene with mud clinging to the sides of the car and caked under the wheel wells. I got the car cleaned up so no one would be the wiser. The next day at school everyone was asking what had happened to the football field, and to our surprise, not a single student squealed.

DRIFTING

WHEN I BEGAN DRIVING IN 1964, GASOLINE WAS thirty cents or so a gallon. At H.L. Mills, five gallons of gas cost $1.65. To put things into perspective, it wasn't until 1966 that I had a job that paid a dollar per hour.

There were a few folks in Hedgesville who tried to stretch their miles per gallon by drifting. The process is simple: when you are going downhill, simply put the car in neutral and let gravity do its thing.

If you had lived in central Oklahoma this couldn't be done, but the conditions around Hedgesville were perfect. From the center of town, Route 9 afforded you the opportunity to drift either west toward Back Creek or east toward Martinsburg. A good drift west could take you all the way to the bridge at Back Creek, but heading east would only get you about a half-mile closer to Martinsburg.

From atop the hill at the high school, you could drift all the way to North Mountain. From there you would find long stretches of rather flat road where you could speed up and then drift quite a distance more. This speed and drift tactic could be used all the way to Little Georgetown and eventually to Dam #5. When driving with passengers, they were instructed to lift their feet up when cresting a hill in the road so the car could drift a little further down on the other side. I assume it was a joke, or perhaps they knew something about gravity that I didn't.

You must remember that traffic was very light in those days, so drifting at very slow speeds didn't cause a traffic jam. Today it would be impossible. I drifted a few times — usually when the gas gauge was well below empty. Others did it regularly, I guess, to save money. Can you imagine the chaos you would create if you tried "drifting" in today's fast-paced world? You'd probably be the recipient of some road rage, along with a certain finger gesture.

—∞∞∞—

1962 CHEVY

AUNT DAISY HAD MUCH LOFTIER EXPECTATIONS for me than did anyone else in my extended family. She wanted me to be a minister even though I seemed to be going in the other direction. She had given me a chest of drawers that had some great value. It was said to be part of a set with some pieces residing in the White House. I don't know if any of that was true, but then again, Aunt Daisy didn't lie. The chest of drawers was very ornately inlaid, and in need of repair. My father knew some antique dealers and when they came to our house they couldn't help but make offers on it. It sat in one of our bedrooms a few years as more pieces of inlay fell off.

When I decided to go to college, I needed a set of dependable wheels, so my parents decided to sell the chest of drawers in order to purchase a car. There was no problem finding a buyer and soon it was gone. With cash in hand, the search was on for a car. Anything had to be better than my '54 Ford, though we had certainly made many memories together.

At Kershner's Garage in Marlowe sat a '62 Chevy Bel Air. It was a green, two-door sedan with a 283 engine and three-speed transmission. It wasn't Chevy's top-of-the-line Impala, but it looked and ran great, and soon was mine. It flew down the road like a bat out of hell, as fast as the speedometer indicated was possible. It was only four years old and had very low mileage. It needed nothing, but that didn't stop me from making a few improvements.

I was working at a garage at the time and took advantage of every opportunity to work on my car. It was tuned up with the best parts I could afford. Having the rear end lifted somehow seemed important, though it did absolutely nothing to make the car run better. Regardless, I purchased and installed some spring lifters. They were oddly shaped aluminum objects that were forced into the coil springs and twisted into position. If installed properly they raised the rear end of the car, giving it more of a drag-racer look.

My car came with a three-speed column shifter that worked fine. That didn't matter because it just wasn't cool enough. I went to Joe the Motorist's Friend, a store in Martinsburg, and bought a conversion kit. Installing it was a major undertaking and required some ability beyond my expertise. With help from a real mechanic, a hole was drilled into the floor and the shifter was bolted into place. One kit was designed to fit many vehicles, so there were all kinds of miscellaneous parts lying around. Finding just the right ones to make it work on the Chevy was an interesting undertaking.

Disconnecting the column shifter was simple. The problem was reattaching the linkage to the new shifter now located on the floor. It took some fine-tuning but eventually it all came together. Now with floor shifter in place, raised springs, oversized rear tires, improved carburetor, and some paint modifications, the car was as tricked out as I could afford. It was ready to take me to college, and I was ready to go.

Leaping Dog, Hidden Skunk

J UST ABOUT EVERY TIME YOU HIT THE ROAD TODAY you return home with a memorable story about something that happened on the journey. We have close calls with other motorists and question their ability to drive. We are confronted with situations that require us to respond quickly. It could be as benign as having to hit the brakes to avoid an animal, or as potentially disastrous as averting an accident. As a seasoned driver your reaction comes almost automatically. For a teen driver, however, most auto-related experiences are a series of "firsts." We react as best as we can, and learn along the way.

While returning to Hedgesville late one evening, such an event happened to me. As I rounded the sharp curve on Route 9 by Miller's Store, I noticed a dog was running along the bank of the road to my left. The bank was about eight feet higher than the road. The dog was chasing my car, a timelessly enjoyable activity for our four-legged friends.

Instead of just ending the chase as was the usual canine rule of engagement, this particular dog jumped off the bank toward the driver's side of my car. I swerved to the right as much as I could, but the dog smashed into the side of my car. I slowed down and watched as it rolled across the highway. In a few seconds it came to a stop and simply got up and walked back up the bank. I couldn't believe it — not only was the dog alive, but apparently it wasn't even hurt! It looked as if it was waiting for the next opportunity to interfere with traffic.

While my focus had been directed on the dog, I wasn't

paying close attention to where I was going. I could see there was no oncoming traffic, but I failed to notice a freshly killed skunk directly in my path. I couldn't avoid it and drove right through its remains. Seeing there was nothing for me to do here, I drove the short distance home. Usually skunk smell diminishes as you get farther from the source, but this didn't seem to be the case in my situation. After I parked the car, I quickly figured out why the smell was still so strong. A large portion of the skunk was stuck to my wheels, hubcaps, and wheel wells.

There was that recognizable black and white fur, along with ground-up pieces of assorted skunk entrails stuck to my car. Well, not just stuck to it, but lodged deep into its nooks and crannies. No matter where the skunk parts were attached, the entire vehicle smelled like skunk. Since it was dark, I decided to wait until daylight to clean things up.

From our house to where the car was parked was about fifty yards. As I walked toward the car the next morning it took only a couple of steps to get a whiff of "Pole Cat." Upon reaching the car, the smell was intense. Seeing it in the daylight was much worse than what I had seen the night before. There was skunk all over the left side of my car, and it had hardened and crusted overnight.

There was no such thing as a car wash in Hedgesville, so it was up to me to clean it. If the weather had been warmer I would have driven to Allensville Ford to wash the car in the creek, but it was late fall and cold. I resorted to carrying buckets of soapy warm water from the house. It was part washing and part scraping. Gloves would have been nice but I didn't have any. The skunk had been eating something with seeds. They looked like grape seeds but I wasn't going to analyze them. After a while the solid components were gone, but not the smell, which managed to linger not only on the outside of the car, but also on the inside.

Skunk smell is the gift that keeps on giving, so I drove to the garage, purchased one of those pine-tree-shaped air fresheners, and hung it on the rearview mirror. With windows rolled down and the fresh scent of pine, things seemed to be returning to normal. The car sat all night with the deodorizer working its magic. The next morning when I opened the door however, it just smelled like a skunk in a pine forest.

If I kept the windows rolled down and the heater up on full blast, you could breath and stay reasonably warm. Tomato juice will remove the smell of skunk from your body, but only time will remove it from your car.

Skylark Bites the Dust

NEW VEHICLES WERE RARE IN MY HOUSEHOLD. I can only remember three, and each new arrival was greeted with great fanfare and treated with kid gloves. My parents would let me drive the family automobile, but not very often. My friend Tommy, on the other hand, seemed to have carte blanche when it came to driving his parents' and relatives' cars.

One evening we were having an activity at school. I believe it was practice for a play. Tommy showed up in his parents' brand new 1965 green Buick Skylark. It was full of that new-car smell. Of course I had to take a good look at it, and Tommy insisted on taking me for a test ride. We drove toward North Mountain and turned onto the road leading to Allensville. He exaggerated every stop and start, showing off how much power the engine had.

This road had a series of very sharp "S" curves. As we approached the first curve I thought he would slow down. Not so. He kept accelerating, only applying the brakes just as we entered the curve. The reality is that we didn't successfully complete any of the turns we were about to enter. Instead we plowed into a shale bank, smashing the front end of the car. The bumper, hood, fenders, and lights were damaged, but the car was still able to be driven.

After concluding that neither of us was hurt, he put the car in reverse and backed onto the road. It was messed up pretty good and covered with dirt and debris. Being only a couple of miles from the school, he decided to drive it back. Even though it was dark and we had no lights, we arrived without incident.

Now came the dilemma of what to tell his parents. For me this would have obviously been the worst part of the whole experience. Not so for Tommy. He decided he would tell his parents he had run over a board in the road that forced him to swerve, thus causing all the damage. I thought it was a lame excuse, but he was theatrical and decided to go for it, and headed home.

The next day at school he was calm and smiling when I saw him. His parents had bought the story — hook, line, and sinker — and there were no consequences for what he had done. He had always acted as if he was smarter and wiser than his parents — both of whom had college degrees. I believe they just wanted to avoid confrontation. His parents were far too intelligent to believe his excuse and Tommy was much too naive to think they had.

———&&&———

THUMBING A RIDE

N EVER DID IT. NEVER NEEDED TO DO IT. I ALWAYS had a car. This was not true, however, for everyone living in Hedgesville. If you had no car, you hitched or thumbed a ride. It's easy to do: when a vehicle approaches you, just stick out your right hand with fingers folded inward, a right thumb up in the air, and move your arm in a motion that pushes your thumb in the direction the vehicle is traveling.

You will know that you've caught the attention and interest of an approaching driver if a car or truck slows down and comes to an eventual stop. At such point it is customary to proceed without haste to the awaiting vehicle, and find out how far the driver is headed in your intended direction. Even if you will not be taken all of the way to your final destination, you will probably be able to get a whole lot closer to it.

The driver may or may not have known the hitchhiker. Regardless, the two usually found a subject of mutual interest to discuss. Hitchhikers couldn't have a strict schedule as they never knew when or if they'd get a ride. I wonder if that fact was relaxing or frustrating to them?

My father used to pick up hitchhikers. Being a male, he probably didn't worry too much about the possibility of something going wrong. In our travels along the miles between Hedgesville and Charles Town, it was common to find someone needing a lift. I gave some rides but really wasn't too keen on stopping for strangers.

On one occasion my friend Tom — not Tommy — and I were driving from Back Creek Valley to Martinsburg on our way to visit our girlfriends. I was the passenger and we were coming up the mountain along Buck Hill. Suddenly a guy with his T-shirt half off flagged us down from the side of the road. We stopped, ready to give him a ride. Being in the middle of nowhere, in the dark, it seemed like the right thing to do.

I rolled down the window and he approached the car and began telling us his story. He said people were chasing him, trying to do him harm. Something didn't sound right, but we listened as he kept talking. I noticed his right hand was partially covered by his T-shirt. Looking closer I saw he was clenching a screwdriver much like one would grasp a knife. As he talked he kept moving his hand until he had freed it from his shirt, and then he pulled it behind his back.

The car doors happened to be locked but the windows

were down. I reached for the knob to roll my window up and told Tom, who was aware that something wasn't right, to floor it. Off we sped with the person running behind us, but we were faster and got away, of course.

I will never know if any of this man's stories were true. Perhaps he wasn't alone. Someone could have been behind a tree or out of view along the road. Was he a hitchhiker, a potential criminal, or both? What would have happened if we stayed just a little longer? I really didn't care as we were long gone and so was he.

THE FLYING PIANO

WATCHING PIANOS ATTEMPT TO DEFY GRAVITY is something I have done more than once. This story is about a piano that tried just that on its journey to Hedgesville.

My father was the only family member who owned a truck. Therefore, he became the mover or hauler for everyone in the family and for some friends as well. On this particular occasion he was asked by a relative to haul an upright piano from Martinsburg to Hedgesville in his 1955 Chevy step-side. This truck was my father's pride and joy.

He had built a small set of wooden racks for it, which was more decorative than functional. He had a large set of cattle racks, but for this trip they were not used.

If you have ever moved a piano, you're well aware that it's as heavy and awkward an object as you will probably ever encounter. At least four people are needed to lift one. Once on the truck, its height measured about four feet above the sides of the truck, and at least two feet above the decorative racks.

Loading the piano onto the truck was uneventful. Its back was against the passenger side of the bed, tied to the racks on that side to secure it from rolling forward or backward. It then began its journey to Hedgesville along Route 9. Slow and steady wins the race, so that's how we proceeded up the road.

Just below the last hill leading to Hedgesville is a sharp, left-hand curve — the site of the leaping dog, hidden skunk fiasco. Miller's operated a small grocery store there for a few years. There was a drop-off of several feet on the right-hand side of the road and a guardrail placed there for protection.

The piano had traveled without incident about half a mile short of its destination, but somewhere in the middle of that left-hand curve, things went terribly wrong. The piano didn't roll forward or backward, but rather flipped over the side of the truck. It bounced off the guardrail and fell several feet into the parking area, landing with an explosion. The wooden cabinet went in all directions and the soundboard, with some strings still attached, did the same. It was the most melodious crash I'd ever heard, and much more interesting than the normal thud usually heard when a large, heavy object is dropped.

No matter how it sounded, this piano was history. The truck, which was unharmed, was stopped and the piano pieces were collected. The assorted remnants of what had just moments ago been a piano were delivered, but were received with great disappointment. Nothing was said about my father covering the loss, just as nothing had been said about paying him for the transport in the first place. The decorative racks were gone; they had entered into the cacophony of flying piano parts.

That event taught me a piano lesson unlike any I had learned as a child: when a piano attempts to defy gravity, gravity always wins.

Hag-Mart

IF YOU LIVED IN THE BERKELEY COUNTY AREA in the 1950s or '60s, just the sound of the word Hag-Mart will bring back some wonderful memories. Almost every sizeable town had its drive-in eatery. Some were established chains and some were independently owned. In addition to the Hag-Mart, Martinsburg had the Arkay. Hagerstown had Richardson's. Winchester had Jumpin J. This was before the time of McDonald's and Burger King, at least around here. Hollywood's version of a cruise-in eatery was possibly an amalgam of bits and pieces of what these establishments were like across the country. What we might have seen on television and in the movies can sometimes muddy the waters of our memories, but I can recall those things that made our cruise-in one of a kind.

The Hag-Mart was located on North Queen Street in Martinsburg. It was a concrete-block building and was painted orange and black — the colors for Martinsburg High School. The exterior walls displayed the menu. Looking through the large, open windows you could see Hires Root Beer barrels and the attendants scurrying around filling orders. The kitchen, located toward the back of the building, wasn't visible to the public.

The Hag-Mart was family friendly. You pulled your car into the parking area which surrounded the building on three sides. Many cars were filled with children as well as adults. Shortly after you arrived, a carhop was at the driver's window ready to take your order. Parents usually knew what they wanted. Not so for the kids. With hands grabbing the top of the front seat, the back seat passengers pulled themselves forward to the open front window to make certain their orders were heard correctly.

The specialties I remember most are hotdogs covered in their famous Hag-Mart sauce, root beer, pork barbecue sandwiches, and the best hand-cut French fries ever made. The root beer was drawn from large barrels and served to you in a frosty glass mug. If by chance they had run out of mugs, the carhop would apologize for this inconvenience. Imagine that! Today they would just say they were out of them and move on. If you wanted root beer to go, they would fill up gallon jugs and deliver them to your car. It was tasty no matter where you drank it.

Their barbecue sandwiches were delicious, piled high with meat, dripping with sauce, and perfectly seasoned. Their French fries were hand cut and fried to the perfect degree of crispness, just right for ketchup dipping. The hot dogs, smothered in secret sauce, were the bread and butter of the place. All of the food was good.

There were no tables for eating. The food was delivered to your car on a metal tray with brackets that went over your slightly rolled-up window. There was an adjustable arm that extended downward with a rubber end cap on it. When pressed against the car door at the correct angle, a level surface was created that held your food.

After paying the carhop you began distributing the food. At that time, cars didn't have cup holders. An open glove box could serve as a tray for the front-seat passenger. This worked fine if it was just you and your date, but not so well for cars with back-seat passengers, most of which were children. They had to just put the food on the back seat, in the rear window, or on their laps. Of course there were many accidents within the car. I never saw a tray fall off of a car, but I feel certain it must have happened on occasion.

The food was also served to go, but rarely did I ever take it home to Hedgesville. I was working jobs in retail stores that stayed open rather late. My steady girlfriend lived in Martinsburg and we had our routine: when I got off from work I drove to her house, picked her up, went to the

Hag-Mart to get our food, and then headed to the drive-in.

Since the Hag-Mart was a cruise-in and didn't have indoor seating, it was not open during the cold months of the year. It must have been difficult to compete with the new wave of year-round, fast-food chains. The Hag-Mart was torn down more than forty years ago and was replaced by a McDonald's restaurant. Fast food had finally arrived in Martinsburg. I feel sure many people thought the arrival of McDonald's was a step up for the area. It may have been to some, but we felt a loss of both our favorite hangout, and our favorite sauce.

With the end of the Hag-Mart era came many attempts to replicate their infamous sauce. Ask ten people who claimed to have the secret recipe and you would get ten different versions of the sauce. Today, most people who prepare it have a backstory that aims to prove their version is the authentic one. However, to dispel all myths and settle all disagreements once and for all, a relative of the owner posted the family recipe on the internet.

Drive-Ins

MOVIES BEGAN SHOWING AT DUSK. IT WAS AS common to arrive after the flick had begun as it was to be there at its beginning. If you arrived late, you carefully drove into the theater with your headlights off so as not to disturb the punctual patrons. You'd search for a perfect spot, which for us was always in the last row, against the fence. We usually had our Hag-Mart food with us, and thanks to our proximity, it was usually still good and hot when we arrived. We ate our food and drank our root beer, and sometimes even watched the movie, but usually not.

We had two drive-in theaters from which to choose — the Sky-Vue and the Pine Grove — and there was always a double feature shown. Drive-ins catered mostly to the younger crowd, though the Pine Grove had a play area directly below the screen with swings for the younger children. There were lots of Elvis, beach, and monster flicks shown. Nobody really cared how good the movies were. We were there to be alone, and I *won't* digress.

The movie was projected onto a large wooden screen. As you rode around neighboring towns, you could always spot a drive-in theater by the presence of this tall object. Audio was supplied by a network of metal speakers. As you pulled into your chosen parking space, you maneuvered your car as close as possible to a metal pole cemented into the ground. A small metal "T" was attached to the top of the pole where two detachable speakers were held. A wire connected the speakers to the pole.

If the metal pole was beside the driver's door, that's the window where you'd attach the speaker. Just the opposite if it was on the passenger's door. The speaker had a bracket that fit over the window. To keep it in place, you rolled up the window, but it always left a gap at the top. Each speaker had adjustable volume control though the sound quality from the small device left much to be desired.

When the movie was over you returned the speaker to its pole before exiting the theater. In the rush to leave, however, some people would forget to remove the speaker and just drive off, breaking the wires. More often the wire was intentionally cut and the speaker was stolen. (I just so happen to have one from both drive-ins, but they were given to me — *really,* they were.)

Sometimes the mad rush to leave the theater happened before the movie ever began. One such occasion was with my usually carefree friend, Tommy. A bunch of us were piled into the 1958 Ford he was driving. There were more people crammed in than the car could safely accommodate. In the back seat was a case of beer that Tommy had purchased. We pulled into the drive-in, found a perfect spot in the last row, and piled out of the car.

Before the flick ever began, a police car entered the theater, drove past us, and circled the grounds a few times. Tommy was sure they were onto him so everyone piled back into the car and we left. Instead of calling it a night, we headed for downtown Martinsburg. We came to a stop at the intersection of King and Queen Streets — the town square. The car behind us was making a loud noise. The driver was revving up his engine, and his exhaust either didn't work or wasn't there. It was loud. Now re-enter the police. They pulled up and approached our car. Quickly the case of beer was covered. The cop thought we were making all the noise, though he soon realized it wasn't our car, and we were allowed to pull away.

We may have missed the drive-in double feature that night, but we all felt like stars of our very own action adventure flick. And who knows — someone may have even gone home with their very own drive-in speaker as a consolation prize.

PART TWO

HIGH SCHOOL

Same Building, Different World

I BEGAN MY JUNIOR YEAR OF HIGH SCHOOL IN 1964. It was in the same building with basically the same teachers I'd had since seventh grade. What was different was *me*. I could now drive to school if I chose to, and it felt like I had so much more freedom. Activities at school and away no longer required parental participation, and how I conducted myself was completely up to me — a point I can't emphasize enough.

The high school was certainly the largest building in our little town. It was a formidable two-story brick structure situated atop a hill. Having only about 350 students, you knew almost everyone. Many of us had younger or older siblings at the school. We did our best to avoid the younger ones as we thought we were so much more mature. School had been and would continue to be the main hub around which most of my activities revolved. It was where I learned, played, and socialized.

As we were in school for the better part of the day, it was only logical that events occurring beyond Hedgesville would be reported to us during the school day. Nothing was happening within a vacuum. We didn't have the twenty-four-hour news cycle that is so familiar to us today, but we did receive information about world events at home from the television, radio, and newspaper. The worlds of home and school overlapped for us, however, and some of the most pivotal and life-changing events in our lives were seldom timed to coincide with the last bell of the day.

In America's race with the Russians to conquer space, Sputnik flew high over Hedgesville as I watched the sky, not actually understanding what was happening. I sat in class and listened over the school's intercom to the broadcast of John Glenn's suborbital flight. I learned in my geometry class one afternoon, just after lunch, that President Kennedy had been shot and killed.

Before this begins to sound like nothing but bad news, I must tell you that high school could not have been more enjoyable. It was a blast partially because of the fact that

I avoided the serious studying part of it until very late in the game. School was like a great adventure with many avenues to explore. You could be nerdy, cool, sophisticated, comical, or just you. I chose the "you" track.

There was a club or organization to cover just about every interest a high schooler could have. We had student council, National Honor Society, Future Homemakers of America, Future Farmers of America, and clubs with specificities like science, Spanish, and drama. There was band, chorus, and a variety of musical subgroups.

Along with the pursuit of talents and interests, there was the opportunity to vie for social status and popularity by gaining titles such as the king or queen of several school dances. We could also compete for very specific titles such as "Mr. and Miss Eagle," named after our school's mascot. Other than a picture in the yearbook, I don't know what perks came with those honorary titles. Some of the other titles up for grabs, which also appeared in the yearbook, included: best all around, most polite, best dressed, best dancer, most dramatic, biggest flirt, most athletic, class nuisance, best personality, wittiest, jolliest (which I was named), and most likely to succeed. We also had senior last wills and testaments, and favorite quotations.

From the time I had marched up the hill from the elementary school and entered sixth grade, to beginning the last two years of high school, my small-town experiences had shaped me. My world was now changing and expanding, however, and I was changing right along with it.

SCHOOL LUNCH

YOU MAY THINK A STORY ABOUT SCHOOL LUNCH couldn't be interesting. That might be true today, but not so when I was in high school. Hedgesville High was so small that when lunch was served, all high school students ate together in one big batch. There was no such thing as a closed campus, so you were free to walk home or visit the local greasy spoon if you wished.

Our school served the same non-exciting meals as did all others schools. Living as close to the school as I did allowed me to walk or drive home quickly, so I rarely ate in the cafeteria. I would either grab some leftovers from the refrigerator or eat a TV dinner which my grandmother would conveniently place in the oven before my arrival. More often than not, lunch consisted of a fat-encrusted piece of meat on a slice of bread.

Eating lunch wasn't the most important activity during this midday time away from classes. Socializing was of utmost importance. Some guys hung out in the parking area behind the school, discussing or sometimes even repairing their cars. Some groups sat on the tall concrete wall running the entire length of the front of the school. The truly "happening place," however, was in our old gym. There was a record player controlled by several girls who had a pretty good supply of popular music.

Essentially, there was a sock hop each day at lunch. Very few slow songs were played and very few boys danced. Mostly the girls danced together, showing off the latest moves they had learned from watching programs such as American Bandstand. The boys sat, watched, talked, and critiqued those on the dance floor. It never got out of hand and needed little supervision. I can't imagine something like this happening today.

Periodically the dance was called off and a movie was shown. You paid a dime or so to watch the flick. They were full-length movies, so it took a few days to see the entire movie. The blinds were shut and we sat staring at the screen, trying to hear the dialog above the noise of the students and the projector. I remember watching *Caine Mutiny* there, among other movies of the day.

If this all sounds very simple compared to today, that is because it was. Rarely were there any problems, let alone fights. We knew how to behave and what was expected of us. Maybe some students were actually hungry for food, but most of us were hungry for entertainment and the chance to show off our social graces, even if they were in desperate need of refinement.

—⚬⚬⚬—

SPORTS

IN MY FAMILY SPORTS WERE NOT VERY IMPORTANT. That's a major admission for someone from Hedgesville. My father had never played any sports, and no emphasis was placed on them. If professional wrestling, however, was a sport, then there *were* sports fans in our house. We watched wrestling on television and even attended a few local events in Hagerstown and Charles Town. This is a bit off track from discussing high school sports, but I must list a few of the wrestling heroes of that time. There were male superheroes such as Gorgeous George, The Graham Brothers, Haystacks Calhoun, Bruno San Martino, and Arnold Scoland — who was almost always defeated.

Beauties such as Slave Girl Mula represented the women. There were even midget wrestlers. I had always thought it wasn't real and seeing opponents arrive and depart in the same vehicle helped confirm my suspicions.

Now, back to high school sports. As a child, I had played sports with my neighborhood friends. I also played church league baseball. In high school I tried out for basketball. It should have been easy because I was tall. Not so. I lacked everything *except* height. Next came wrestling — not the pretend kind — but *real* wrestling, which was extremely demanding. Unfortunately, I weighed enough to be placed in a category where my opponents were much larger than I. They looked like giants. Again, I saw no future here.

Track and field was another adventure. I can't recall ever competing in an event, but I did give it some practice time. Pole-vaulting was attempted using an aluminum pole with absolutely no flexibility. I quickly realized that was not for me. Shot-put seemed simple enough. We practiced in the unfinished basement area under the new science wing. All I can say is, look out steel rafters! Discus was attempted with little success. Several of us even "borrowed" the discs from school and practiced in my garden. Sadly, no Olympic potential existed for my friends and me.

Then there was football. Being big was an asset. If you were alive you made the team. I guess I played just to be part of the gang. It was okay, but I could live without it. The two-a-day practices in August were killers. You would sweat so much it was hard to separate your clothing from your skin. We were short on equipment but pieced enough together to field a team. To say we were not very good was an understatement. This, however, did not stop students from paying the small amount of money needed to get out of class and attend our games — most of which took place during the second half of the school day.

The high school sat atop a hill. To the east were terraced areas containing the ball fields. The football and baseball fields shared a terrace. One end zone of the football field was the infield of the baseball field. The terraces were narrow — not much wider than was required to contain a football field. If you "shanked a kick," the ball would go over the bank into brush, sometimes never to be seen again.

During football practice we ran laps. The backstop for the baseball field was at the north end of the football field and we were to run behind it as a part of our lap. Our coach couldn't see very well. Groups would take turns stopping behind the backstop, while others would take their turn running. The coach just saw a group of boys running, never knowing the actual number in the group. The fact he had difficulty seeing was great during practice, but terrible on game day. He usually kept someone nearby on the sidelines to count the number of our players on the field so we would not get penalized. It didn't always work.

I gave up my football career, deciding my time could be better spent elsewhere. If you look at a yearbook from this time period you will see the hard-core sports enthusiasts who played multiple sports. With such a small population to draw from, many students starred in football, basketball, *and* baseball — the holy trinity of high school sports. Many of these athletes dated cheerleaders who were also majorettes. I had other interests and found myself slipping away from the sports scene. It probably worked out better for everyone.

DONKEY BASKETBALL

TO SAY THAT OUR OLD GYMNASIUM WAS SMALL IS an understatement. The actual court area was not anywhere near regulation. There were two rows of bleachers on the sidelines, and those sitting on the first row would essentially have their feet on the court. Passing a basketball in from the sidelines meant, unfortunately, that your rear end was in the face of someone sitting on the first row.

One day the game was changed a bit, and into our cramped gymnasium entered eight or ten teachers and students on the backs of donkeys. Many of the participants had never ridden a horse — other than one on a merry-go-round — let alone a donkey. The donkeys involved were under the supervision of a company that was traveling a circuit in the area.

The opponents were usually faculty verses students, and the goal was to do exactly what you did at a regular basketball game, except to do it from the back of a donkey. Did I forget to mention there were no saddles? The legs of some riders were so long that their feet were dangling only inches above the floor. Most riders tried to lock their ankles under the belly of the donkey to gain more stability.

Staying atop the donkey was the first mission. Balance was critical. Holding on to the ball with one hand while guiding the animal with the other was next to impossible. To the benefit of the players, the donkeys rarely raced off with any speed. It was usually just the opposite, and getting them to move at all was a challenge. If one did happen to bolt, it would then abruptly stop wherever it wanted, usually without warning, and cause the rider to slip off and hit the floor. As spectators, that is what we wanted to see. Participants were to move toward the basket, shoot the ball, and score some points. Very few points were scored.

Watching the event was hilarious. Large animals and inept riders do not mesh well and the results were quite entertaining. Of course there was also the occasional donkey bathroom break — always a high point of the competition. It's a wonder no one was seriously hurt, including the spectators whose feet were directly in the stomping zone.

I haven't heard of any such event in the area for some time. Perhaps they are gone forever. If animal rights advocates were concerned the donkeys were somehow hurt, they may have been focusing on the wrong animal — humans got the worst of it in donkey basketball.

THE PIANO MAN

THIS STORY BEGAN AS AN INNOCENT PHYSICAL education class in the old and very small gymnasium. Its overall length was about half of what a standard gymnasium should be. It was also extremely narrow, with two rows of bleachers on either side, and a stage at the far end. You entered the gym through multiple doors on the main level of the school. The entrance directly in front of the gym led to the main entrance into the school, and was adjacent to the principal's office. This fact is important to note, along with the fact that the gym had a hardwood floor and masonry walls.

During one gym class the instructor was summoned to the office. He instructed us to sit on the bleachers and remain quiet. On the stage was an upright piano. It sat near the front of the stage, just a few feet in front of the closed curtains. Theater lights were positioned at the very front of the stage. They were attached beneath hinged, hardwood panels that allowed the lights to be recessed into the stage floor and be practically invisible when not in use. Unlocking them with an Allen wrench would allow the several-foot-long panels to be flipped up, revealing the multi-colored lights beneath.

On this particular occasion a student decided to leave the bleachers and go to the stage, even after being told to sit still. He proceeded to open the piano and attempt to play something. The stage lights were in the closed position so they just appeared a continuation of the stage floor. The problem was, although the panels were closed, they had not been locked down. After his impromptu performance, while walking off the stage, the student gave us an encore we wouldn't soon forget. He stepped onto one of the light panels and it flipped open, causing him to lose his balance. Rather than falling to the floor some three feet below, he made the unfortunate decision to grab the piano.

What happened next was like one of those moments when you are witnessing a nonpreventable accident — you can't stop looking, and everything appears to be happening in slow motion. A bleacher full of classmates watched on as both the student *and* the piano fell off the stage onto the wooden gym floor. Luckily he wasn't hurt, but the piano wasn't so fortunate. It made an unbelievably loud crash, echoing off the masonry walls and wooden floor. Ebony, ivory, and wooden pieces flew in all directions, and the soundboard cracked, allowing wires to escape.

In a split second, or so it seemed, the student got up and rejoined us on the bleachers. He was sweating nervously. The sound had caused the principal to run the few feet from his office to the gym where we all sat with mouths wide open. The principal first surveyed the remains of what had been a black upright piano, now in pieces on the gym floor, and then he turned his attention to us. The impromptu pianist was sweating even more by now and we didn't think the principal would have any trouble figuring out that he was responsible.

Instead of going to this nervously sweating student, he stopped in front of me and asked me if I was okay. I of course, said "yes," wondering why I was being questioned. He pointed to my head and asked me how bad my head was feeling having just been hit by a falling piano. I didn't quite know how to respond. I said nothing and he again expressed concern for the red mark on my forehead. It was then that I realized he was referring to my birthmark. The principal had known me all my life, living just down the road and attending the same church. He certainly wasn't discovering this for the first time. After a moment he realized his error and began inspecting the others sitting on the bleachers.

By now our piano player was sweating profusely and finally caught the principal's eye. I'm not sure if a confession was made, but the culprit had been identified, and I was off the hook. I still wonder how the principal could possibly think a piano falling several feet off a stage would only leave a red mark on someone's forehead. If it had hit someone on the head there would have been human parts mixed with the wood, strings, and ivory laying on the gym floor, and the victim would most likely not be sitting on the bleachers.

What would be the punishment? There certainly was no code written in the administrator's handbook to cover this situation. The punishment ended up being simple: the student was to reassemble the piano. Of course he couldn't rebuild it to a usable state. His job was only to make it resemble a piano again, and he sat in the corner of the gym with glue for days trying to do just that.

I don't remember how many days he labored, but it probably was not for too long. Did he learn anything from this incident? I learned two things: a piano falling from a stage onto a gym floor produces an unbelievably loud noise; and a principal who had known me all my life had never really taken a close look at me.

HIGH SCHOOL ROMANCES

WHAT, I ASK, WOULD HIGH SCHOOL HAVE BEEN without romances? There comes a time in almost everybody's teenage life when the facts of life cannot be ignored and you search to find the perfect mate. In the small town of Hedgesville, students had attended all grades together from elementary to high school, so we had observed each other at length and knew each other rather well. At some point along the way, as if Noah himself had called, pairs were formed among the student body. Athletes found cheerleaders. Cool guys found cool girls. Bad boys found bad girls. Even nerds — though the term didn't exist then — found their romantic counterparts.

I didn't try to pigeonhole myself into any particular category. I was neither a jock, nor cool, nor bad, and certainly not a nerd. I had only a few dates early on in high school, and they were just to sock hops and Fun Night. No serious love connection was made until I did a rare and unspeakable thing for that time — I ventured outside of the community.

While most of the guys attending Hedgesville High School were dating their classmates, one friend of mine decided to date a girl from Martinsburg. They went out a few times, but there was no mutual interest. When I got the free and clear, I decided to give her a call. We also went out a few times, and just like my friend's experience, there was no mutual interest. It was on my last attempt to ask her out one November evening that fate intervened and the course of my life was forever changed. During that one last phone conversation she expressed such complete disinterest in me that she handed the phone over to her cousin.

The cousin — whom I'd never met — said her name was Gula, but I thought she said "Beulah." I had not heard of the name "Gula" up until that time, and haven't since. After we got the name thing sorted out, she kindly explained why her cousin was taking a hiatus from the dating scene. She also told me that if I ever wanted to call her instead, that it would be fine. She gave me her number and about thirty minutes later I called. We talked for more than two hours.

During the course of our marathon conversation, this sixteen-year-old boy from Hedgesville got up the nerve to ask her out, and she said "yes." She was only fourteen years old at the time, so our first date was simply meeting at her home. I knew from the moment we met that she was the one for me. We dated from November of 1964 until June of 1969, but it was not until she turned sixteen that I was allowed to transport her in my car. When she visited me in Hedgesville, or when we went out somewhere, it was in the parental shuttle, and under strict parental supervision.

It might have been easier for the couples who attended high school together in Hedgesville, but I had my true blue girl in Martinsburg and she was well worth the wait. I wouldn't have had it any other way.

— ✦ —

THE DEEP FREEZE

I BELIEVE EVERY FEMALE AT HEDGESVILLE HIGH was required to take some form of home economics class from our one and only home economics teacher. She was not young, and appeared more like a grandmother figure than a teacher. I guess she had ample life experience to teach all the skills necessary to be a homemaker. No males took this class and rarely did they venture into this domestic territory unless forced to do so.

The home economics classroom was always tidy, and had tables set for fine dining. The kitchen areas were very modern looking. It was in this classroom that many freezers were located. They were not the upright kind, but rather were chest freezers, and were packed tightly with all kinds of goodies. The not-too-well-kept secret was that the goodies were also well aged.

Lots of baking must have taken place within these walls, and by the look of the freezers, there was more production taking place than actual consumption. Just about any food that could be frozen was. In order to rotate the inventory, the teacher would serve from the bottom of the freezer. The newer, fresher, top items were removed, the lower items were retrieved and thawed, and the top items were repacked. As guys, we only knew about this inventory management system because we were drafted to lift and carry the items.

Home economics food was served at most school functions and especially at dances. It was readily available, aged to a sort of perfection, and catered by a teacher who was always eager to attend these affairs. Truth is, it would not have surprised me one bit to be carrying a cake and upon reading the label, see my mother's name as the person who had baked it years before.

Fun Night

THAT WAS THE NAME GIVEN TO AN EVENT THAT happened each fall at our school. By today's standards most students would be hard pressed to see anything fun about it. For my generation it was fun. The gym and several classrooms were transformed into activity centers for just one evening. We purchased tickets that could be used for any of the activities. Of course, there was also home economics food available for purchase.

Cakewalks were held in the gym, and there were games of chance similar to those at a carnival, but with a slight twist. While most of the prizes offered at carnivals were stuffed animals, the prizes at Fun Night were *live* animals, including fish, kittens, puppies, ducks, and chickens. I don't know what the mortality rate was once the animals left the school, but it was probably rather high.

The highlight of Fun Night was always the sponge toss, or more accurately described, the sponge "throw." Various faculty members suited up in whatever rain gear they had, and took turns sitting on a stool. Sponges were pulled from a bucket of water and then thrown at them. Here was a chance to show how you *really* felt about your teacher. Macho guys would throw as hard as they could. When a direct hit occurred, they would smile and look around, anticipating great support from the crowd. Their expression would change from one of great accomplishment to something much less if crowd support didn't materialize. I guess it wasn't as satisfying as they had thought.

In one room at the end of the hall you could hear music playing. It was coming from a record player. This was the room for dancing. I was not then nor have I become a great dancer. I couldn't see wasting a ticket here. The room still looked like our social studies classroom with the desks just pushed aside. It had no atmosphere.

I always think Fun Night must have been such an exciting outing for my mother when she had attended the school so many years ago. The event silently passed away before I graduated. At this period in time, fun was taking on a totally different meaning. School was losing its place as the focal point for activities. My wheels now afforded me the opportunity to expand my entertainment horizons to neighboring towns with more to offer.

∞

SCHOOL DANCES

ALWAYS ANTICIPATED WITH GREAT EXCITEMENT were high school dances. We of course had proms, Homecoming, Valentine's Day, and any other holiday dance we could squeeze in. We even had a Sadie Hawkins dance. All were important in their own right.

Most dances required minimal preparation and had little fanfare. If we wore a tie or sport coat we considered it a sophisticated event. If a corsage was ordered, the event was elevated to a much higher level. A corsage meant your date was wearing a fancy dress, and you had to have prior knowledge of its color before ordering. Complicating this more was determining whether it would be worn on the dress or wrist. Such pressure for a teenage boy!

The Sadie Hawkins dance came with its own peculiar rules. Girls were to ask the boys out. There were rarely any surprises as you usually attended with your regular date. Dress was completely different. Bib overalls and cut-off shorts with loud plaid or polka dot patterns were the norm. Vegetable greens tied together made the perfect corsage. I'm sure our version of this classic dance was very different from its origins, but for us it was a lot of fun.

The junior-senior prom was the pinnacle of our school dances. There was an unwritten, but collectively understood protocol for this event. You and your date made the perfect plans for the evening. For guys the first thing you did was clean the car. No matter what condition the car was in, it now got washed and polished. You then ordered the flowers from a florist in Martinsburg, as Hedgesville had none. Next you chose the restaurant for your pre-dance dinner. Many people formed groups for dining, which only complicated the logistics.

It was our tradition that the junior class planned and

executed the prom for the seniors. The juniors selected the theme, decorated the old gymnasium, organized the refreshments, and planned the music. Most dances had music provided by a record player but for prom we hired a band. Choosing the band was my job. I felt so important.

Let me take a minute to describe how the gym was transformed for prom. The junior class, in my case all thirty-three of us, would spend several days decorating according to the chosen theme. With ladders, tape, scissors, and an abundance of crepe paper at the ready, we began stretching streamers from the perimeter of the gym to the center of the ceiling. The problem with stretched crepe paper is that it just keeps on stretching over time. By the evening of the prom, many of the streamers sagged so low they'd hit you in the head. There was no way to prevent this; it just happened. Tables and chairs were added and before long a magical ambiance was created. The gym was off-limits to the seniors until the evening of the dance though most of them caught a sneak peek beforehand.

Car and body now cleaned up, prom night arrived. Off you went to pick up your date, present her with the corsage, stand in a location chosen by her parents, and have your pictures taken. Oftentimes prom portraits were staged at both your home and your date's. Next we proceeded to dinner, which was usually at a restaurant we had rarely if ever been before. We ate our dinner while discussing everything that had occurred in preparation for the evening. We felt so sophisticated. There was an air of excitement for what the rest of the evening held in store.

You never arrived at the prom at the very beginning. Oh no, the moment of your entrance was carefully timed. Throughout the evening we either danced while ducking streamers, or sat back and critiqued everyone else. We were treated to some of the "aged" refreshments from the home economics deep freeze.

I vividly remember one prom having a Romanesque theme. There were columns made from the large cardboard tubes used at Dupont to hold dynamite. A local department store loaned us manikins that we draped in togas, adorned with purple plastic grapes, and placed on the stage among the columns. I used our limited prom budget to hire The Bill Krantz Orchestra, a five-member band whose bass player had made, from scratch, an amplified, stand-up base guitar. The band was situated on the left side of the stage. I don't know why so much attention was spent creating this scene, but it was. Despite our best efforts, however, the results looked less regal than anticipated, and more like the scene of a Roman orgy.

During the course of the festivities, one student felt the need to touch one of the nine-foot-tall columns, which was attached to the stage only by cheap tape. As he touched it, they all began to fall like dominoes. When the dust settled the area looked more like Pompeii than Rome. It didn't matter that we had just witnessed the "fall" of the Roman Empire because we were at the prom. How could you possibly improve on an evening such as this? We were all dressed up, our dates were adorned with flowers, and we were dancing and ducking streamers. All of these factors combined made a wonderful experience.

When the prom was over there were some parties you could attend, and as a senior it wasn't uncommon to stay out all night. My girlfriend, Gula, and I went to one at a cabin along Back Creek near a local swimming hole. Some people arrived already quite inebriated, and several bottles of cheap champagne were being passed around. That wasn't our scene, and we left shortly after our arrival. Most people stayed out until the wee hours of the morning and then returned home to sleep late into the afternoon.

———

PARTIES

I CAN ASSURE YOU, WHAT WE CALLED A PARTY would not even register on today's party scale. All we needed were a few people, some snacks, some soda, and music. Not every element was necessary as long as there were people. Some homes were just better suited for parties than others. Mary Kate's and Tommy's were the best, perhaps due to the lack of parental interference.

We didn't have alcoholic beverages and certainly no drugs. In fact, I don't ever recall seeing or hearing of drugs in high school, though alcohol was readily available. A record player provided the music of the day, including songs such as "The Night Has A Thousand Eyes" and "Go Away Little Girl." Our parties were nothing more than gatherings with no real rhyme or reason. They were relatively calm and never truly got out of hand.

Mary Kate's house was within walking distance to mine. Her parents never seemed to mind us teenagers hanging around. Her mother mostly stayed in the kitchen and her father usually was not home. They never seemed to care who was coming or going in and out of their home. I remember someone asking her mother for a needle and some ice, which she provided, totally unaware that someone was about to get an ear or two pierced.

Mary Kate's house was even older than mine. Though it had indoor plumbing, its toilet was only accessible by exiting the house on its east side, re-entering through an exterior door, and descending to the basement. There it was — a throne in the truest sense — as the toilet was placed atop a wooden platform. Interesting to say the least.

Tommy's house was a stately mansion, and equally old. It was a three-story, stone structure built by Hessian soldiers. The rooms were filled with expensive antique furniture including a grand piano. A modern apartment had been added above the kitchen and was where his aunt resided. Upon her passing, it became Tommy's lair.

His family also stayed away from our gatherings. His mother taught school and his father was a gentleman farmer. Tommy was, to say the least, eccentric. He lived in a world of his own. He reasoned in ways I can't begin to understand. There seemed to be no oversight from his parents, and I don't think he was ever told "no."

On one occasion a group of us were hanging out at his place and decided — for reasons I can no longer fathom — to make lasagna. Not just any lasagna, but a *huge* lasagna.

To our surprise, the kitchen was stocked with all of the ingredients we would need. We didn't double or triple the recipe, but went for a sort of "ounces-to-pounds" ratio. This conversion produced a final product that was monstrous, twenty-six-pounds, and very savory. There were enough leftovers to last a year. "Go big or go home," as they say. We went big, and the lasagna went home.

<hr />

TYPING CLASS

LONG BEFORE THE DAYS OF COMPUTERS AND WORD processing, we had typing class. Not keyboarding, but typing class. It was an essential class for future secretaries and was highly recommended for those planning to attend college. There was no studying or homework involved, so it was an obvious choice for many of us!

Our typing class was held in the bottom level of the school in what had once served as the cafeteria. I don't know what qualifications were needed to become a typing teacher, and we really didn't care. Our instructor happened to be the wife of the principal, and a familiar face around our small town of Hedgesville. In fact, many of our teachers were local residents who sometimes attended the same church as your family and shopped in the same grocery store. Perhaps this fact kept us a little more honest, but far from perfect.

Most of us took typing class expecting to get an easy, good grade, and maybe learn to type a little along the way. But the less typing we had to do, the better. To this end we could usually manufacture some kind of distraction in which to involve the teacher. Typewriter ribbons made for a good diversion. We could always run the ribbon to its end on the spool. The ribbon was supposed to reverse, but when pushed down with some pressure could be intentionally locked up. Up went your hand, the teacher would arrive, and before long she would be all inked up. This would successfully bring the class to a complete halt.

Our typing books were long and rectangular. You opened it up and flipped it over to view the passage to be copied. Our exercises were timed, and when the teacher told us to begin, we'd type our fingers off. Of course, you were not supposed to be looking at the keyboard. We were scolded every time she observed us doing it. When told to stop, you began counting how many words you had typed and the number of mistakes you had made. This is how you calculated both your words per minute, and your grade.

A classmate sitting beside me had a system guaranteed to always give him a high number of words per minute without any mistakes. He would, in advance, type a portion of the exercise on a clean sheet of paper and place it inside his desk. He would do this while we were supposed to be practicing. After the class had completed several minutes of practice, we were instructed to insert a new sheet of paper and wait for the timed exercise to begin. It was at this time that my classmate would slowly insert his pre-typed paper into the machine. If he never typed another letter on it he was insured of a good grade. When the class began typing, he would type very slowly and carefully. He never made a mistake because he had ample time to visualize each letter before striking the key. His words per minute were high and his mistakes were next to zero. He got great grades but never really learned to type.

My typing skill far exceeded that of my "hunt and peck" buddies. Ends up that typing "THE QUICK BROWN FOX JUMPS OVER THE LAZY DOG" — the sentence using every letter in the alphabet — proved an asset in college and beyond, and made writing this book a whole lot easier.

Yo No Hablo Español

I F YOU TOOK A FOREIGN LANGUAGE CLASS AT Hedgesville, you took Spanish. We were told we needed two years of foreign language if college was in our plans. I hadn't seriously decided if I would go on to college, but I went ahead and took Spanish just to cover all of my bases.

Our school building was old, but for some reason we had a modern facility in which to learn Spanish. It was called a lab and had a central control console from which the teacher could monitor each student. Students wore headphones and listened to audio played by the instructor through the console. We were to either respond to, or repeat things we were hearing. The instructor was rather interesting, but lacked basic classroom management skill. He seemed intelligent, but, come to think of it, I don't ever recall hearing him speak a lick of Spanish.

We had homework assignments of which most were translations. I thought they were rather boring and tedious in nature. The problem of doing them was solved when I found out my girlfriend was taking Spanish at North Junior High School in Martinsburg. She was conscientious about her work and good at Spanish.

I started giving all of my homework assignments to my girlfriend and she would carefully complete them. I would pick them up, take them to school, and then share them with anyone and everyone. We all got good grades but learned very little Spanish. I hate to say it, but I learned little more than how to count from one to ten.

The irony of the story is that my wife and I have dear friends in Spain. We visit them and they visit us. My wife can converse with them to a degree in Spanish, while I am limited to "Please pass the bread and butter" and, of course, counting to ten. Many years have passed since Spanish class and my wife is still doing my translations.

Don't Let the Cat Out of the Bag

DISCLAIMER: IF YOU ARE A TRUE, HARD-CORE animal lover, skip this story and move on to the next. I really mean this, as you might find everything about it wrong on so many levels. However, if you continue to read on, please be advised this was not a hurtful prank. It was what we were instructed to do by our teacher. If you must lay blame on someone, lay it at her feet.

Dissections are very important in the understanding of how organisms are put together and function. General biology students dissected worms, crayfish, and frogs. Junior- and senior-level anatomy and physiology students dissected *cats*. For me a cat was just a cat. We had them as pets and we accepted their life cycle.

There always seemed to be a giddy, nervous excitement about dissecting anything, especially something the same size as your family pet. Perhaps students in larger cities rarely saw dead animals. I know that in some schools today they do what are called "paper dissections." Comparing a cat to a human is a far stretch, but I would want the surgeon operating on me to have seen and handled more than a paper-doll version of a human. I don't think playing the game Operation qualifies anyone to be a doctor.

By the mid 1970s, biology class specimens were ordered from a supply company and were delivered to the school preserved and ready for dissection. During my high school years, however, things were a bit more "hands on." Our teacher stated that we would begin dissection after each two-person lab team got a cat. You guessed it. We were to find our own specimen, and it was to be neither a living nor a flattened, road-kill specimen. This would not be a problem, as cats were readily available and we just had to select one.

Nobody, of course, wanted to volunteer their family pet for the project. A friend told my lab partner and me about a lot of strays hanging around his barn. We could come and choose one, and so we did. With burlap bag in hand we grabbed the first available feline. The next stop was the home of my lab partner, Susanne.

We didn't want to be cruel to the animal and pondered what would be the most humane form of euthanasia. The problem was solved not by us, but rather by my partner's mother. It wasn't a method that gave us any joy, but rather what an adult parent told us to do. I won't get into the details, but the process involved the cat, a burlap bag, a metal can, and the exhaust pipe of a '59 Chevy. It was quick, and relatively painless, I hope.

At school the next day our cat was placed into a plastic bag and put into a refrigerator along with others. Now we could begin our study of a mammal in a scientific and respectful manner. There's a twist to this story, however. Our teacher fell ill and took an extended leave of absence.

We had barely even touched the cats at this point, and our substitute teacher wasn't about to delve into dissection, so the cats remained in the refrigerator for a rather long time. As our specimens — which were not vacuum-sealed as they are today — began to swell and smell, the substitute told us to get rid of them. Those instructions were quite vague and left a lot of room for interpretation, as there was also no oversight provided.

Several of us decided to take the smelly, dripping, bloated bags from the fridge and head over to the far sidelines of the football field. Beyond the sidelines was a steep drop-off covered with weeds, brush, and small trees, with a farmer's field just beyond. One by one the bags were flung down the hill toward the field. None made the full journey, as the bags — many only loosely tied — opened up and released their decomposing contents. The smell was awful and it wasn't a pretty sight to see. Avoiding getting "cat soup" on you was a major priority. When the task was complete, we went back to class. More bookwork followed, and all dissection ceased.

Please don't make rash judgments based on what you have just read. Today, no teacher in their right mind would ask their students to do what we had to do. Their teaching career would be over and all parties would have a criminal record. It was a different time and place and many things were accepted that today would be unheard of. Remember, this was a time when there were few seat belts or car seats for children, and anyone could sell you cigarettes. Attitudes and protocol have changed, thankfully.

DROPPING PENCILS

A S TYPICAL TEENAGE BOYS, THERE WAS ALWAYS an overpowering attraction to the opposite sex. We didn't have it thrown at us on television or movies as it is today. Of course there were magazines and books that left little to the imagination, but nothing beats the real thing.

We had a young female teacher, which was unusual. Most of our teachers were much older, had established families, and usually lived within the community. The fact that she had little teaching experience was one strike against her. The second strike was the fact that she wore loosely knit sweaters that offered a glimpse of her supporting undergarments. Yes, it does not take much to get teenage boys excited very quickly.

Our teacher would walk around the room and lecture us on chemistry. To our great fortune, her classroom had hightop lab tables and stools rather than the usual desks and chairs. Sitting on tall stools expanded the distance from the desk to the floor. If you happened to drop a pencil onto the floor just as the teacher passed by, she would pick it up and hand it to you. While bending over she would inadvertently reveal an even greater view of what her undergarments were supporting.

To this end you would often hear the sound of perfectly timed pencils hitting the floor as she patrolled the room, followed by the sight of a head bending over to watch her make that glorious retrieval. It was a pleasant distraction, harmless entertainment, and undoubtedly provided a first-hand chemistry lesson that we wouldn't soon forget.

Throwing Keys

WE'VE ALL HAD THOSE MOMENTS AS STUDENTS when we sit in class and our minds leave our bodies for a trip to another place. It is usually a short trip and we quickly return. We had a science teacher who apparently didn't like to see us take such journeys. He had a large ring of keys that he kept handy on his desk. If he observed you "mentally leaving the classroom," he would pick up those keys and toss them at you. You could be hit in the head, chest, or any other part of the body, or just be startled as the keys hit the desk or floor next to you. Since this teacher taught many of the classes in the science curriculum, his students became slow moving targets from year to year. You couldn't really avoid his aim until graduation.

———<del>◦◦◦</del>———

CHEWING GUM CHAINS AND TIN FOIL

G UM WAS CHEAP — JUST FIVE CENTS A PACK. This was a real bargain as a stick could last several hours. Your choices were varied and included Doublemint, spearmint, peppermint, cinnamon, and my all-time favorite, Juicy Fruit. We were allowed to chew it in class and when it lost its flavor, it was often deposited under our desks.

There was more than one benefit you could derive from chewing gum. The wrapper, after packaging and protecting the gum, could serve another useful purpose. Female classmates sought out the outer paper wrapper with its colorful advertising. They folded it in a particular manner and connected it to others folded likewise, forming long, continuous chains. What the final product was to be, I haven't a clue. Perhaps the chains just got longer and that was the reward in itself.

There was yet another use for a portion of the wrapper. Inside the paper wrapper the gum was protected by an additional two-ply sheath: thin paper lined on the outside by the world's thinnest layer of aluminum foil. Trying to separate the foil from its attached paper without tearing it was your goal. If you ever completed the task, you had a small, rectangular, useless piece of foil.

It wasn't the piece of foil, however, that we were most concerned about. It was mastering the skill required to obtain it. Remember, this was happening during class when we were supposed to be learning important things. Instead, we were determined to master the rare and delicate art of foil removal, however useless it would be in advancing our careers in the world beyond high school.

<hr />

HE GOT HIT BY A BEER TRUCK

THIS ISN'T REALLY MUCH OF A STORY, BUT AT THE time it just seemed like the coolest thing to say. For some unknown reason the phrase *"he got hit by a beer truck"* worked its way into any conversation we were having. I don't know its origin, and I can't recall anyone actually getting hit by a beer truck.

For a period of time it was our answer for any question to which we could insert it. If the teacher asked us where someone was, they would hear, "He got hit by a beer truck." The phrase rapidly gained universal use among us. It fell out of fashion, however, as quickly as it had arrived, joining a long list of colloquialisms that can be used to date periods of time. I'm sure more phrases will come and go. "You can bet your sweet bippy!"

SMOKING IN THE BOYS' ROOM

THAT JAMES DEAN COOL LOOK DIDN'T EXIST AT my school. Jeans were worn, but they were the type worn around the farm. T-shirts were an undergarment only visible around the neck area. Never were they worn as an outer garment. You never saw a pack of cigarettes strategically rolled up in a T-shirt sleeve, either.

Smoking wasn't allowed in school, but this didn't stop or even discourage some from sneaking a smoke during the school day. I can honestly say I was not a smoker. I did try it once, but found no pleasure in it at all. For those who did, the coolest place to smoke was in the restroom, even though you would always expect a faculty member to visit during the class changes. Perhaps it was the excitement found in trying to beat the system that made the activity even more tempting.

Since the restroom provided the most privacy available in a public school building, that's where smoking was done. Sometimes a guard was stationed outside the restroom door, but most often it was every man for himself. Taking as many drags off of a cigarette as possible in only a couple of minutes caused a blue-gray haze to loft toward the ceiling. Even if you didn't smoke, you reeked of it by just being in the restroom.

The fact that a faculty member had entered the restroom could be confirmed by the sizzling sound of cigarettes being extinguished in the urinals and toilets, the instant flushing sound, and quick exit by the student. Some guilty parties would go so far as to keep the smoke in their mouths until the coast was clear. Another method used to avoid detection was to curl your fingers inward, hiding the cigarette in the palm of your hand, or even putting the lit cigarette into your pocket. I don't actually know how successful any of these tactics were.

When a new wing was built onto the school, a restroom was located adjacent to the cafeteria. There was a metal grill near the ceiling, supposedly used for ventilation. On occasions you could look up at the grill and see eye movement. There was a storage room on the other side, so access for viewing was readily available. I don't know if we were being watched, but rumor had it that the principal would crawl up there to catch smokers.

⸺◦◦◦◦⸺

ONE MAN'S TRASH,
ANOTHER MAN'S TREASURE

THERE IS A PRETTY GOOD CHANCE THAT MOST students get an opportunity to cheat on a test or homework assignment over the course of their academic career. Copying a report almost verbatim from an entry in the encyclopedia, or looking at your neighbor's test paper for a few answers, might be at opposite ends of the spectrum, but they are both cheating. I wasn't the world's greatest student, but I didn't find it necessary to cheat in order to pass a class. That doesn't mean that I was above using an opportunity to my advantage, however.

This brings me to a particular class. I must first describe the circumstances that led to this opportunity. There were some students in school who worked in the office as aides,

– 89 –

performing various functions. One such function was to operate the mimeograph machine and duplicate tests and worksheets. This task was done in a small room next to the office. There was a door that connected this room to the main hall. Once the duplicating was completed, the masters were thrown into the trash, along with any rejected copies. We were on the honor system so, in theory, the room was secure and off limits.

On one particular occasion it seemed as if we were almost entrapped or set up. Let me set the scene. It was late spring and the seniors were about to leave on their class trip. One senior aide had been making copies of a test that she would not be taking, but that the rest of us juniors would. The test was for a class that had been a struggle for almost every student. Most of us were passing, but by the skin of our teeth.

Before leaving for the senior trip, the aide told a classmate that she had placed several copies of our next exam in the trash can, should we choose to retrieve them. Someone — I really don't know who it was — did so and word spread quickly among us students. At lunchtime it was agreed that those interested would meet on the stage behind the curtain and get a leg up on the test, which was scheduled to be given that afternoon.

We met and "studied" as a small group, sharing only with those in our inner circle. When it was time for class, we entered the room and saw our sad-looking teacher standing together with the vice principal who was left in charge for the day, as the principal had gone with the seniors on their class trip. They asked us a few questions, ultimately ending with who had seen the test.

Most — but not all — of the guilty raised *our* hands, and were immediately marched off to the vice principal's office. We sat there and when we had the room to ourselves, we discussed how our plan had gone so terribly wrong. We quickly learned that one student who had been excluded from viewing the test ratted us out. Excluding that student was our downfall.

We sat and waited for the administrator's return. When he did, he began questioning us as to how this whole thing had happened. We said nothing. This was our new plan — not to play ignorant, but to just keep silent. He told us that we were likely to be suspended from school for a period of time to be determined by the principal upon his return. Until then we were to sit in the vice principal's office and think about our misdeeds.

This should have made us feel awful, but for some reason we didn't view our act with the same degree of seriousness he did. To that end, the next day as we sat and supposedly thought about our crime, a deck of cards appeared. When we were left unsupervised, we played cards. A rather long time passed until we eventually got caught, and from then on we just sat and grinned at each other, occasionally laughing out loud.

When the principal returned to school, he and his proxy must have spent some time discussing the event. The principal thought we had been punished enough, so we were permitted to return to class. I don't remember our parents even being called, for if they had, I would have faced some serious consequences.

The only truly awkward moment was when we returned to class. Our teacher just stood there and asked us why we had made such a bad choice. Again, we remained silent. We weren't about to rat out the senior aide who made this whole thing possible, and we certainly were not going to criticize the teacher for failing to impart the knowledge needed for the course, which is ultimately why we cheated in the first place. The moral of this story is to not cheat. However, if you do, make certain that everyone is involved.

— ∞ —

NOVEMBER 22, 1963

THERE WILL ALWAYS BE MONUMENTAL MOMENTS in your life that will stick with you forever. Ones such as the lunar landing and the first moon walk were joyous. Ones such as the shooting of President John F. Kennedy, and other tragedies since, haunt our memories.

On this particular day in history, after lunch, I was sitting in geometry class on the second floor of the high school. A student who had gone to the front office returned, bursting into the room with news that President Kennedy had been shot. We didn't know what to think because we had no access to any further information. About an hour later, our principal delivered the somber news over the intercom that the President of the United States was, indeed, dead.

Upon arriving home we watched the news with Walter Cronkite as the story unfolded, and expected the worst. On Sunday morning I sat in front of the television and watched — live — as Jack Ruby shot Lee Harvey Oswald, the accused killer of the President. It was a confusing series of events to witness as a child, and still today I can't really put these events to rest.

Where were you when President Kennedy was shot?

SCHOOL PLAYS

HEDGESVILLE HIGH SCHOOL PRODUCED ITS FAIR share of plays, and they were as far off-Broadway as you could possibly get. I don't recall the names of many of them but I do remember a few. We performed "A Christmas Carol," and some lesser-known plays, including "Fanny The Frivolous Flapper" and "Three Pink Leprechauns."

Chains were needed for "A Christmas Carol." The only chains we had were a set of car chains, so that's what we used. As for the play "Three Pink Leprechauns," there was a need for lots of pink paint and cloth. Pink paint could be mixed at a paint store; pink cloth was another matter.

We solved the pink cloth dilemma by simply buying lots of pink Rit dye and a huge amount of white cheesecloth. These items were loaded into the car and we headed for Martinsburg, the nearest town having a laundromat. The first step was to ignore the large signs telling patrons to not put any dye into the machines. Next you added twice as much dye as was instructed on the package. Finally, when the machine stopped, you quickly grabbed your very pink material, closed the lid, and made a hasty retreat. One can only imagine what the next patron thought upon opening the lid and seeing the pink interior of the washing machine. Hopefully they looked inside before tossing in their laundry.

I acted in a few of the plays and helped out on a few others. It seemed we were into recycling before it became fashionable. One of the sets was being repurposed for use in, I think, the Charm Queen competition. "Little Shop of Horrors" was popular at the time and one of the sets had a large window drawn on it. It only seemed logical for us to rename the store "Mushnick's Flower Shop," so those large words were painted on the set. Those who were actually in charge thought otherwise, and it was changed to "Café Le Fleur." Mushnick's still seemed the better choice. The painted flowers still remained but Audrey had to go. If you've seen the movie, it will make better sense to you.

There was a one-act play competition held at Shepherd College. We ranked high enough to be sent to the state competition at West Virginia University. A group of us traveled there and stayed at the Mount Chateau. I can't remember anything about the play or the competition. What sticks in my mind is listening to the only popular song the hotel lounge had on its jukebox, which was "Viva Las Vegas," and walking across the bridge at Cheat Lake in the early morning hours.

No one from my class ever became a professional actor or actress. No one went to Hollywood. Those school plays were just diversions in our progression to becoming adults. We learned a little something from everything we did. My theater experience taught me something practical: to avoid laundromats whenever possible, and when not, to check twice and load once.

THE LIVING NATIVITY

THERE ARE A FEW CHRISTMAS PAGEANTS HELD in the area today, and some churches still display a traditional manger scene with a makeshift stable, a few animals, and some humans dressed in appropriate costume. None of these, however, compare to the rather elaborate production I participated in as a teenager.

Our Nativity scene wasn't held in or near a church, but on the outskirts of town, along Route 9. A working farm owned by the Linton family became, for one weekend, the venue for our large-scale rendition of the Christmas Story. The stable scene was re-created in a barn on the property. An abundance of hay bales were strategically arranged to disguise the barn's modern appearance. The open fields provided a perfect outdoor backdrop for our performance. Since it was a farm, there was also no shortage of animals. Ours was a *living* Nativity in the greatest sense of the word.

The event was not sponsored by one church, but rather by the entire community. There were dozens of participants both in and behind the scene. The milking parlor served as the staging area where we were fitted with costumes — most of which were held together by safety pins and string. We wore layers of clothing underneath to stay warm.

People often say it was colder and snowier when they were young, and I have to agree. There was usually snow on the ground, transforming the cornfield into a rather desolate-looking landscape. If you had the part of Mary, Joseph, or a Wiseman, you were afforded some protection from the elements because most of your time was spent in the barn. Even though it was completely open on one side, it was warmer and less windy than in the open fields. I was always a shepherd, which meant leaving the warm milking parlor and heading out to a designated rock ledge in the field well before the program began. Our sheep went along with us, even if they didn't particularly want to.

Spectators could either park in the field and stand around the front of the barn, or stop along the highway and view the event from their heated cars. A public address system was used to narrate the performance, so being near the barn wasn't really necessary in order to hear what was going on. There weren't speaking parts in this performance anyway — only gestures relating to the story.

As shepherds, all we had to do was stand in the dark and wait for our appearance in the pageant. We were such a distance from the barn and the audience that we could talk about anything, but we mostly rocked back and forth and complained about the cold. We often didn't listen to the narration but took our cue when a large spotlight was directed onto us. That meant it was time to look up in amazement and begin leading our sheep toward the barn. We walked a few yards in that direction and then the spotlight was redirected. We were done for that show. The problem was, we couldn't leave the scene even though we were now not a part of it. It would have been a distraction to the program. So again, we stood in the dark and waited.

When the play was over, we made our way back to the milking parlor. We warmed up, drank hot chocolate, ate some cookies, and took any necessary bathroom breaks — a particularly challenging feat due to the layers of clothing and costume. It was only minutes until the next showing.

Refreshed and warmed up, we went back to do it all again.

I wish a program of this magnitude could be brought back today. The site is still there and our community has grown in numbers, providing many potential participants. The highway is too busy to have people park along it, but the field is still available. Advancements in winter clothing would sure make it a lot more comfortable to be a shepherd.

Marching Band

FOR SUCH A SMALL HIGH SCHOOL WE HAD A FAIRLY large marching band, though it wasn't the top priority organization in the school. Athletic teams were number one, or so it seemed. The jocks received elevated status and individual praise. Not so for the tuba or trumpet players.

The guitar was my instrument, but I never saw one in a marching band. I could play a little piano, but again, not a marching instrument. I tried my hand at trumpet and could hit a few notes, but it took too much practice. How about drums? That was my answer! I could play them and almost no practice was required. My plan wasn't unique as there was an abundance of people who could pound. Being able to also read music was a plus. Snare drums were number one, followed by tom toms, and last but not least — the bass drum. I didn't care which one of them I played and had a turn at all three. Later on our school received a set of tympani drums. They became my instrument of choice and even made their way into parades. It was unique at the time, but common today.

Bands seemed to center around their director. Some directors were very strict and stuffy, and then there was ours. He was different from us and most other directors, and that was a good thing. He was very innovative and always had new ideas for doing things. He didn't live in Hedgesville, but rather came from Martinsburg. He drove a cool car, and dressed likewise. Our band director was definitely what you would call a hipster.

Rather than talking *at* you, he talked *to* you, and he was able to play a variety of instruments. His age wasn't much above the seniors, but he seemed to have acquired a world of experiences, which he frequently shared with us. When I say "us" I don't mean the entire band. Most band members were hard at work learning music and behaving properly. Then there were the drummers.

Our band room was a metal outbuilding adjacent to the school. It had once been an agriculture and shop classroom.

It was hot in the summer, cold in the winter, and could barely accommodate the entire band during practice. We drummers avoided the band room whenever possible.

Our band didn't have the support behind it that exists in today's school bands. There was no booster organization of parents who found themselves just as involved as the students. There was no comfortable, fancy, charter-style bus dedicated to transporting the marching band unit, nor was there a large truck with trailer to follow us to and from parades. We piled all of our instruments into the back of a school bus and we piled ourselves into the front.

We practiced for parades by marching up and down Route 901 which ran adjacent to the school. We would line up in front of the school and make a left-hand turn onto the road. There was very little traffic and any vehicle at our rear inadvertently became part of our impromptu parade. The town porchsitters knew approximately what time the band would be marching by, so they sat and waited for their afternoon entertainment. We marched down the hill to Poisal's Store and right beyond — at the intersection of Routes 9 and 901 — we turned around and began our return to school. Today that would be a death wish even with the addition of the traffic light.

We played halftime shows for the football games. We practiced themed shows like the ones you see today, with orchestrated movements choreographed to the music. This was fairly innovative for the time, and we had our band director to thank for it. He had us play traditional march music, but he also added many of the popular songs of the day to our repertoire, including "Block Band Jazz," "Cotton Candy," and "Java," as well as Sousa marches.

In addition to marching band we had jazz band, another brainchild of our director. It was in this group that I finally got to play my guitar. We also acquired a stand-up bass and I gave it a whirl. We played at various school functions and assemblies. My high school music education helped in the formation of my first rock-and-roll band.

∞

PARADES

JOINING THE MARCHING BAND WAS SOMETHING I did just to have fun. The atmosphere surrounding the band was carefree and happy. Sports seemed to be much more serious. They were always competing and there had to be a winner and a loser. We competed but actually never lost anything.

Marching band offered opportunities for travel. Parades in neighboring towns meant a bus trip without parental supervision. There was a degree of freedom and adventure that made those uncomfortable bus rides seem fun. Parades were the time to show off our unique talents, and each town we visited had a uniqueness of its own.

Front Royal, Virginia, hosted a small parade just a little over an hour away from school. We were running late as was often the case, and upon our arrival the bus driver just stopped in the middle of the road and we unloaded. The parade had already begun so we ran down several blocks, attempting to get dressed and find our place in the marching order along the way. On this occasion I was playing a bass drum and was having some trouble getting the canvas harness attached while running down the street.

The band formed up and began marching while I was still trying to get everything attached. The snare drums joined in but there was no bass. The drummer next to me noticed my predicament. He decided to play my bass drum for me as it was waving around in all directions while I was desperately trying to get it fitted. He had no mallet so he used one of his drumsticks, immediately slicing through the head of the drum, tearing it wide open. Two drumheads are necessary to produce the desired sound. I now had only one. I marched the entire length of the parade with my drum producing a unique sound much like someone pounding on a bag of potato chips. I might have pulled this off if our band had been playing a traditional march, but we weren't. We were playing one of our cool new songs that relied heavily on drums, and it was obvious that we were one big drum short.

The route of the parade held in Hancock, Maryland, provided the opportunity for our band to march through a town as well as under a bridge. This parade took place in the fall and sometimes it would be quite cold. Some of the town folk viewed the parade in a completely different light. They would perch themselves atop the bridge and see us as moving targets when we emerged from underneath. Their weapons of choice were water balloons and assorted fall fruits and vegetables. It was like the terrible troll in reverse, and left us a mess by the time the parade was over.

The Mummers Parade in Hagerstown, Maryland, had been a tradition since 1921. It was then, and still is, a large parade happening around Halloween. On one occasion we decided that certain beverages might keep us warm as we marched. Several jugs of hard cider were purchased and brought on the back of the bus. The bus ride to Hagerstown was about forty-five minutes. A handful of us drank the jugs dry during the short trip. We stood around for what seemed like an eternity, waiting to begin marching. The parade route was long and there were no restrooms for us to use. We were getting sicker by the minute, and after a terribly uncomfortable march we made our way between any available buses in the parking lot and began relieving ourselves in various ways, depending on how sick we were. That was the last time I ever drank hard cider.

The biggest parade we marched in was the Apple Blossom Parade in Winchester, Virginia. This was a two-day event, with the Fireman's Parade on Friday night and the grand feature parade on Saturday afternoon. Our band director had an idea: since we now had tympani drums, why not put them into the parade and I would play them! In order to do this, the shop class had to build a cart — not just any cart — but rather a chariot of sorts on which to place the drums, that could be pulled by several students as I walked behind. At least our band director didn't consider using real horses. As I said, he was cool, not eccentric. This was unique and no one else around was doing anything like it. Hurray for little Hedgesville!

The cart had a U-shaped cutout toward the back where I was to walk. It put me in the perfect position to play the drums located at either side, but having their forward movement controlled by someone else presented some complications. Bands move as a unit, receiving direction from the drum major. It normally works well, and if you stop a little late, it's no big deal as there is space between you and the row of people in front of you.

Having the drum cart directly in front of me eliminated wiggle room. If the pullers stopped short I'd run into it; if they stopped late I would run into it. You guessed it — I was always running into the cart. Its base was several inches above the ground, just about shin level. The set up was a hit with the crowd, but when the parade was over, my bloody shins revealed that it was also a "hit" with me.

After completing our march we headed back to the buses to store our instruments. We then had some free time to roam around. Not really paying attention to anything in particular, several of us walked past a convertible parked on the side of the street. There was someone sitting in the car in usual parade position. I saw this person's hair and started staring, as it was a strange shade of red. I quickly figured it out — it was Lucille Ball!

She did not appear in real life like the "Lucy" I knew from television. Of course ours was black and white, but I had seen her in the movies, in technicolor. She looked very different in person. She didn't seem happy or funny, nor very attractive up close. Again another image shattered, and both having a Winchester connection. Years ago I had a similar reality check when meeting Winchester native, Patsy Cline, in my living room.

THE 1964 WORLD'S FAIR

OUR BAND DIRECTOR WAS ALWAYS ONE STEP ahead of the game. In 1964 the World's Fair was being held in New York City, which might as well have been on the other side of the world from my standpoint. It was a place I saw on television and read about in magazines. I never thought I would see it up close and in person.

We became aware of a competition being held from which bands would be selected to play at the World's Fair. I don't know if it was a local or national competition, but we practiced and practiced, made a recording, and sent it to be judged. This was a big thing in its own right. One song we played was "Theme from the Apartment."

I'm not sure if anyone thought we would be selected, but we were. Some bands were chosen to stroll around the fair and play music at no particular venue. Others would perform concerts at specific sites, and that is what we were chosen to do. The problem was how to pay for the trip, as being selected did not come with financial support. Our director again worked his magic, soliciting donations from any source he could find, and raising enough funds for all of us to make it to The Big Apple.

The male members of the band stayed at a YMCA in Manhattan, which wasn't as fun as it might sound. Every morning we ate breakfast, schlepped to Times Square, boarded the Flushing-bound number 7 train, and headed to Flushing Meadows where the event was being held. The elevated subway ride was fascinating, providing a bird's eye view of ethnic communities and sites I'd never before seen.

We entered the fair over a very wide, wooden bridge. Directly in front of it was a huge metal globe of the earth. We walked down an avenue and headed to the West Virginia Pavilion with our eyes and mouths wide open. This wasn't your average county fair. The pavilion was elaborately designed to resemble a coal mine. Our instruments had been shipped to the site and were waiting for us when we arrived. We played several concerts there but had an even greater honor: performing at the United States Pavilion. In addition, we went to the RCA Studio and recorded some songs that would later be broadcast at the fair.

We had a good deal of free time to wander the venue, which was a fair, carnival, and circus combined. I was able to visit pavilions from other countries and see many large industrial exhibits. At the General Motors Pavilion the song "It's a Small World After All" played continuously as visitors toured the exhibit from a moving, car-like ride. Sinclair Oil Company had a "Dino" mascot that was large enough to walk through.

There was an amusement area with rides and plenty of food. They even sold beer. We, of course, had to have our fair share of all the concessions, and we probably had a bit too much before our recording session. The intensely hot lights and cramped studio space didn't jive with what we had consumed. The hotter it got, the more the beer and hot dogs "fermented" in our stomachs. Needless to say, the lengthy subway ride all the way back to Times Square was very uncomfortable.

A few of us spent the night sitting on the shower room floor, trying not to get sick. Our principal who had come along as a chaperone wandered into the shower room to find us in various stages of misery. When asked what was wrong with us, someone replied that we had all eaten some bad hot dogs. He bought it.

We left the city with some wonderful memories and a few we would have rather forgotten. Many of us had purchased kazoos shaped like trombones. We played the most stupid songs on them and must have driven the bus driver crazy on the trip home.

That was my first trip to New York City, but it certainly wouldn't be my last. I would return again in just two years for my senior class trip.

⤫

CHORUS

FOR A SCHOOL AS SMALL AS HEDGESVILLE HIGH, we had almost every opportunity offered at much larger schools. "Mixed Chorus" was another venue through which students could express their musical talents, and opportunities abounded for the chorus to perform at school. Like our band director, the chorus teacher was not afraid to take a leap of faith and attempt to develop every little bit of available talent.

Our chorus programs were nothing like they are today. We had no dedicated room to practice, but instead just occupied a corner of the old gymnasium. There was no live orchestral accompaniment, but rather just an old, upright piano in need of tuning. There were no try-outs. If you showed up, you were a member. We had no choreography, but rather just stood still and sang. Rarely did we perform beyond the walls of the school other than at a choral festival at Martinsburg High School. It was there that we sang with other county school choruses, assessed our level of talent by comparison, and decided to do more practicing.

Getting new music was a luxury seldom experienced, so we sang standard tunes such as "He," over and over again. For one concert our teacher decided we should have solos. Mine was "Call Me Irresponsible." Much like our band instructor, our chorus instructor tried to be innovative and follow current trends.

Folk music, or "hootenanny" music as it was sometimes referred to, became vogue. As a guitar player, this seemed like a good thing for us to try. A few members of the chorus formed a folk group, with me accompanying on guitar. We sang at a few events in Martinsburg and even performed at the local canteen.

For such a small school, I was given a shot at many musical activities and learned a little from each of them. I guess I was about as well-rounded in my music education as I could have possibly been. From tonette to tympani, and everything in between, music was a very important part of my school years.

FOOD POISONING

G ROWING UP I WAS FORTUNATE TO HAVE BEEN rather healthy. There were multiple bumps, scrapes, and a few stitches, of course, but there were no broken bones or major traumas — only the usual childhood maladies such as measles, mumps, and chickenpox. I did have my appendix removed at the age of four, and took my turn at a town game I like to call "pass the hepatitis."

During my senior year of high school, a group of us students from Hedgesville, along with other schools, went to Shepherd College to participate in a seminar on world affairs. There were speakers and small group discussions on current events and world politics. The topics weren't the most interesting, but it was enjoyable because we were at a college and away from school and the usual routine.

I'm not certain exactly what we were to bring back from the experience, but I happened to bring back food poisoning. There are mild and severe forms of it. Some cause discomfort for a day or two, and some last longer. Mine was the latter.

My case was so bad, in fact, that I saw our family doctor and next saw the inside of a hospital room. When we use the expression "sick as a dog," I don't know exactly how sick the dog actually is, but I don't think he could have felt worse than I did. Not only was I unable to eat, but even the smell and thought of food caused my stomach to play the game of "reverse digestion." For days there was no intake of solid foods and the only liquid that made its way into my body was delivered via an intravenous tube.

I was hospitalized for two weeks, and while occupying a double room, I had the opportunity to spend a portion of my stay next to Tommy. I don't remember why he was hospitalized, and he didn't appear ill, but it seemed no matter where he was, his behavior was consistently strange and unusual. He required constant activity. This was well before the days of televisions in hospital rooms, and we didn't even have a radio to entertain us. Tommy acted like a 33-RPM record playing at 78 RPM. None of his actions made any sense. He decided that the ceiling light was dirty, so he stood on the bed, stepped onto a rolling cart, dismantled, and cleaned the fixture. He also thought that the windows needed cleaning, and decided to wash them both inside and out. Hospital windows were operable for ventilation, as there was no air conditioning at this time, so Tommy sat on the sill and hung out of the window, cleaning it with water and toilet paper. He was discharged before me and my hospital stay then became much calmer.

By the time I had returned home and recovered completely, I had lost a total of sixty pounds. Fortunately, food poisoning doesn't leave long-lasting effects, but for me, however, it did. After dropping down to about 160 pounds, I have remained at that weight for my entire adult life. If someone tells me they have tried everything and just can't seem to lose weight, I have to disagree. Obviously they have never tried food poisoning.

———∞∞∞———

SENIOR CLASS TRIP

I AM NOT SURE IF OR WHEN THEY FELL OUT OF style, but for us in 1966, the senior class trip was our final reward for completing twelve years of school. Ours was a trip to New York City. How cosmopolitan I was becoming. I would now be visiting The Big Apple for a second time in only three years! As usual, the only limiting factor was money, but I had been saving up for months.

We traveled on a bus that wasn't painted yellow. It was comfortable, and had air conditioning and a restroom. We were even treated to a stop at a roadside attraction called "Roadside America," which still exists today. We had a guide and other chaperones. The journey there was filled with anticipation and only one problem that I can remember. Somewhere along the way in Pennsylvania a student realized he had forgotten to bring his money. After his initial panic subsided, the problem was solved when the chaperones — prepared for such an event — produced enough extra money to help out my classmate.

We motored into New York and arrived at the *luxurious* Taft Hotel. We had only a few minutes to check into our assigned rooms before gathering back on the bus to begin our tour. Boys were put together on one floor and girls on another. Why was it necessary to separate us from people we had known all our lives? And were we not to realize that the elevator and stairs connected all the floors? There were boys from a military school staying in the hotel at the same time as our class. It became apparent that some of our girls needed to be separated from them.

Once we had all reconnected on the bus, we set out, savoring every sight. First stop on the tour was the United Nations. It was an interesting place to visit, but wasn't at the top of my list of sights to see. I would have appreciated it much more today — age does that to us. I did buy some stamps there which I still have today. It wasn't because I liked stamps, but rather that they didn't cost much.

Next came Chinatown. This place was very different from anything I had ever seen. We were ushered into a storefront and past areas filled with many colorful items, all of which were for sale. Most were either red or gold. A shop employee gave a short talk. It must not have been too memorable because I can't recall any of it, and didn't purchase a souvenir there either. The smell is what I remember the most. The stale air had a complex aroma with notes of incense and urine, but mostly just urine.

Upon leaving there we took a short walk to capture the flavor of the city. I vividly remember one sight: two very intoxicated men trying to cross a busy city street. Their pants were halfway down their legs. For every two steps forward they took at least one step backward. Trying to step up from the street to the sidewalk curb was a major undertaking. We all laughed at their antics. It looked like a comedy skit right from a movie, but this was real. I had seen a similar version of this back home in Hedgesville, but somehow watching these New York City drunks kept me spellbound.

Next stop was a planetarium. We walked there as a group, going through Central Park after dark, and being followed by some unsavory characters. The planetarium was very interesting. We saw some very large meteorites. I had seen some shooting stars in the sky, but this was my first opportunity to see and touch one up close and personal.

One touristy thing we did was to take a Circle Line cruise around Manhattan. The tour lasted a few hours and allowed us to see the city from a different perspective. From the water the skyline was stunning, but some of us were more curious about what we observed in the river below. Several of us noticed condoms floating in the water around our boat, and our new game was to spot and keep count of them. Remember, we were teenage boys.

All tourists visiting NYC had to visit the Empire State Building, and we were no exception. From its top you get a real idea of the composition of the city. The contrast between large concrete buildings and the sprawling green of Central Park was pronounced from our vantage point.

We toured a television studio and ended up at Radio City Music Hall. The performance was just amazing. The organ appeared from a side of the room and the sound it produced was unbelievable. The Rocketts did their show, which was like nothing I had ever seen before. There was even a movie included in the show, called *Arabesque.*

Free time was then given for us to explore. I can't imagine chaperoning students today and just turning them loose in Manhattan. We walked to Times Square, stared up at the billboard of a smoking cigarette, and strolled past clubs. We could watch ladies dancing on top of the bars and hear live music. I don't think we would have been allowed to go in, but there was little need to do so — the doors were wide open and so were our eyes. I remember standing outside of the "Metropole Café" as well as clubs that later appeared in both *Midnight Cowboy* and *The French Connection.* We went upstairs in one establishment and played pool. I didn't do much shopping, but I did buy my girlfriend, Gula, a dress.

We returned home with less money, but a lot more memories. Hedgesville was becoming much smaller to me as my horizons were broadening. I knew the end of something was happening — the end of my rather small, somewhat isolated world. I was about to reach out and grab some new experiences.

I never thought I would return again after that, but little did I know I would become a regular visitor, and return to the scene of my high school adventures.

My daughter had been attending college in Savannah, Georgia, but for her junior and senior years transferred to The Cooper Union for the Advancement of Science and Art in the East Village neighborhood of Manhattan. After graduation she lived and worked in New York City for eight years. When we visited her, she gave us an insider's view of the city that I had only seen as a teenage tourist.

Her last apartment was about a half-block from the number 7 subway stop at the Court Square station in Long Island City, Queens. I had been through that stop many times in 1964 on the way to Flushing. We boarded the train and took what for me was like a journey back in time to the site of the 1964 World's Fair. It's now the Arthur Ashe Tennis Complex, but the iconic Unisphere and a few other structures remain. I again walked down that long avenue.

As we rode the number 7 train back toward Manhattan, we stopped at the various communities along the way. I finally got to experience the sights, sounds, and flavors of those exotic places I was only able to get an overhead glimpse of some thirty years before.

∞

THE PROBLEM WITH TURNING EIGHTEEN

ENTERING INTO MY EARLY TEENAGE YEARS HAD done little but qualify me as a teenager. In fact, it mostly gave me more opportunities to disagree with my parents and those in authority. Age sixteen ushered in a time of greater freedom as my parents began relinquishing some of their control over my life. My newfound mobility brought with it a major shift in how I viewed the world, and also how others viewed me.

Age seventeen offered little change in how I conducted my daily life. I was a junior in high school and couldn't wait to become a senior. There was still a feeling that I wanted to rush things forward. As the age of eighteen approached, however, world events became more important in our everyday lives. We were being exposed to images of war on television and in the newspaper. You couldn't ignore them.

War was something we had viewed in movies or heard about through the stories told by veterans. This was about to change, as our country was at war in a place we knew little about. For a time you could give it a cursory look, but the closer you got to age eighteen, the more real it became. Disturbing images and escalating body counts were being reported on the evening news. More young people were being sent to places with strange sounding names. Our country's involvement in this conflict was deepening, and I was approaching the age where my personal involvement in it might be as well.

To any young man in 1966, turning eighteen marked a significant event in your life — you had to register with the government and the local draft board. The word "draft" is such a simple sounding word, but with such potentially life-changing consequences. Registering meant you were now included in a system that allowed the government to call on you to serve on active duty in one of the branches of the military.

Males who were in high school when they turned eighteen received a card from Selective Service reflecting a deferment until graduation. Males attending college at the age of eighteen were given another deferment, but with stipulations on attendance, course load, and minimum grade point average.

The card came with instructions to carry it with you at all times, much like you would carry a driver's license. Its presence in our back pockets was a constant reminder that the course of our lives could be diverted in a very dangerous direction at the pleasure of the United States government.

PART THREE

ROCK AND ROLL

GARAGE BANDS

MUSIC PLAYED A BIG PART IN MY CHILDHOOD. No one else in my immediate family showed any interest in either listening to, or playing music. How it became such a part of my life, I will never know. It just happened. What began as a plastic guitar under the cherry tree led me to adventures I would never have expected to unfold. From a country music group to various incarnations of rock bands, many memories were created.

It isn't possible to list the names of all the people I met and played music with during my high school and early college years. My friend, Scott, and I were the core of most groups and played music together into our freshman year of college, but he left college and joined the Army.

The Beatles were hitting the airways in the early '60s and we didn't want to be left behind, so we did our best to get a group together. Our first group was formed and we played a talent show at school. The program called us "The Hedgesville Beatles." In the 1960s, anyone who could play four chords was considered a musician. Add drums and amplification and you had a band. They were often nicknamed "garage bands" because of where they practiced and where some should have stayed.

We were your basic garage band and covered everyone else's songs with very little original music. We pieced together an old public address system and got a couple of microphones. Scott had a complete set of royal-blue drums. By now I had retired the old Montgomery Ward's guitar and bought a three-pick-up Kent. I also purchased a new, 150-watt Sound brand amplifier with twin reverb. Playing loud was no longer a problem.

Surprisingly, Scott and I were actually pretty good. We were on the same page when it came to music, and both worked hard at it. His house became our practice place. We rarely used sheet music, but instead I would hear a song and figure out the chords by ear. If we couldn't discern the lyrics, we'd consult song books at the local music store.

When we had enough songs under our belt we hit the road, not knowing if anyone would be interested in hearing us. Ended up they were, and soon we began playing events. We played anywhere anyone would have us. Youth group meetings at churches were popular gathering places for local teenagers, and we were invited to play at a few of them. I think the adult leaders didn't know how to handle this new rock-and-roll phenomenon, so we served as lab rats for their social experiment.

We played private parties, company parties, union halls, school dances, sock hops, and any public venue we could find. We even played the festival circuit where I had once played as a member of a country band. In later years we progressed to some local clubs and bars. I must say up front that if we had depended on the income from the band to stay alive, we would all be dead. Payment for performances, minus the cost of equipment and the investment of time spent in practice, divided by the members of the band, equaled a very low hourly wage. This fact didn't matter to us, however, because at the heart of it we were having fun.

Professional musicians could write volumes of stories about their experiences performing and on tour. We were small time, but not without our own share of adventures.

———∞∞∞———

Practice

Y OU HAD TO PRACTICE AS OFTEN AS YOU COULD and wherever you could. Scott was the drummer and his home was used most often. Perhaps that was because he had the most cumbersome equipment to transport. In our early days we didn't have an organ or it would have ranked the highest in transportation priority. In later years organs were replaced by keyboards and were as easy to transport as a guitar.

We wrote little down relating to musical arrangements. Most rock-and-roll songs weren't too complicated. I could put the chords together and with the help of a music magazine or book could get the exact words for each song. If things got too difficult we'd invade a music store and look at the sheet music. We never bought the sheet music; we just stared at it long enough to memorize everything.

Finding a place to practice could sometimes be a problem. Rock-and-roll bands are loud. Instead of seeking an indoor location, one solution was to take the practice outside. At times this was done in Martinsburg on the back porch of my girlfriend Gula's house. We simply set up and used the porch as a stage. The neighbors didn't seem to mind. In fact, they would show up with lawn chairs to enjoy the free performance. A gentleman showed up one evening and attempted to play the spoons with us. That was an interesting addition to a rock-and-roll band.

BAND MISCHIEF

BAND PRACTICES SOMETIMES WERE THE GENESIS for other adventures. At times it was necessary to visit a music store in Martinsburg, usually to buy accessories or have equipment repaired. Once we got to town we just had to cruise the main drag. There was a man who hung out, or in fact, just roamed downtown. He could function but had some obvious mental issues. I'm certain he got picked on and bullied, and he acted defensive. As we passed him we'd slow down and yell out of the windows with loud voices. He would look wild and agitated, and yell back at us a string of unintelligible words. This seemed like harmless fun at the time, but is certainly unacceptable today.

On one occasion there was a circus at the Berkeley Plaza Shopping Center. This shopping center was where it was happening at this point in time. The downtown was being replaced by these shopping meccas. Band members had all piled into a car for a trip to town. Heading back to practice, we turned north onto Route 11 at the overhead bridge.

Someone in the car suggested we turn into the shopping center. The driver did, and at a rather high rate of speed. The speed was too great and with the sounds of squealing tires and scraping metal, we finally slid to a stop near the circus entrance. The commotion was great enough to cause those in the circus tent to come out and see what was happening.

We were the cause of all the commotion, and thought the experience was quite funny. We were laughing out loud and taking pleasure in what had just happened. That all changed when we were greeted by a security officer who was certainly not laughing. We quickly changed our tune as he explained to us how we had endangered many others with our antics.

All we wanted to do now was leave, but he began to take names and explain what the consequences of our adventure could cost us. He said he was going to send in a report to his supervisor, so we began negotiating for lesser charges. One person even went so far as to ask him if we could have clemency. I don't know where that came from and I'm not even sure he knew what the term meant. We eventually left wondering what our fate would be.

Ends up that this security officer was just a private person hired by the shopping center to patrol the parking area. He had no real authority. In fact, it was later discovered that this was just a part-time gig for him. He actually worked with a parent of one of the guys in our band. Nothing ever came out of this and I just consider it very lucky that no one in the car or circus tent was hurt.

SHENANIGANS WITH SCOTT

SCOTT AND I COULD ALWAYS FIND A WAY TO GET into trouble. I blame it all on him, of course. There was a time when he lived on a farm in the Greensburg area just east of Martinsburg. Some nights I would stay at his house and all we wanted to do was get cleaned up and go visit our girlfriends. Scott's father had other plans for us. He worked at the local bakery and brought home truckloads of old bread to supplement the feed their cattle received.

The bread was piled up on the floor of the barn, and the cattle were on a level below us. We were told to feed the cattle some of the bread before we left for town. In our hurry to get away, only some of the bread was removed from its plastic wrapping. We simply pushed the loaves over the edge to the waiting cattle. I guess they were hungry because they ate all of it. It didn't cause any immediate digestive problems, though I don't know how they handled the plastic. We didn't think this through before we acted.

Another time at the farm, we were instructed to clean a piece of machinery before heading out. It was a manure spreader, or what we called, "The Shit Flinger." It had years of crusted manure anchored like barnacles to every nook and cranny. A fresh coat of the bovine's best, which added odor and texture, hid this crusted layer.

We worked for hours with hammers, chisels, and putty knives. It would have taken years to clean this beast but evening was quickly approaching and we needed to leave. We promised his father we would finish it later. We got cleaned up and headed out. The task was never completed. We couldn't really see the point, to be honest.

Once while Scott was living along Route 9, we decided we needed to go into Martinsburg for some reason. The problem was that Scott had been instructed not to do so. I can't remember how we thought this was all going to work out, but we left the house in an old International truck. Instead of driving the few miles directly to town, we decided instead to take the back roads. This would allow us to avoid his father if he was returning home along Route 9. What were we thinking? If his father came home and the truck was gone, we were in big trouble. That part of the equation didn't even enter our minds.

Off we went in the old International with its cattle racks and an unsynchronized transmission. It also had very distinctive welded metal bumpers. After driving many unnecessary miles on back roads, we approached the intersection with Route 9. We had probably driven ten miles, but were only about two miles from where we had departed. While sitting at the intersection waiting our turn to pull out, Scott's father drove by. The truck was easily recognized and Scott was in trouble again. This journey was doomed to fail from its inception.

After a practice at his home one evening, I loaded my amplifier and guitar into the old 1954 Ford. Scott got into the International truck to leave for somewhere. I pulled forward and he backed up. The front end of the Ford was no match for the metal pipe bumper of the truck. He hit close to the center of the hood and grill, forcing the fenders and lights to turn inward. I now had what I referred to as a "cross-eyed Ford." Both headlights still worked but now illuminated a single spot a few feet in front of the car.

<hr />

DRUM ROLL

NOTHER INTERESTING MISHAP OCCURRED AFTER we played a function at a private club. We had loaded the drumset into Scott's car and were headed home. Today, a drummer packs each drum separately in a protective case for transport. Not so back then, or at least it wasn't so for Scott. He just placed the drums on the backseat and we were on our way. As we were making our way through downtown Martinsburg, we rounded a corner — perhaps a bit too quickly — onto King Street, and one of the back doors of the car flew open. The drums made their exit from the car with a bounce, and began rolling down the street. We pulled over, stopped the car, and ran, chasing them down one of the busiest streets of Martinsburg. Eventually we caught all of the sparkling, royal-blue, runaway cylinders.

<hr />

STAGE WITH A VIEW

T ONE PRIVATE CLUB THERE WAS AN ELEVATED stage at one end of the hall. The restrooms were located at the opposite end on a balcony much higher than the stage. A set of steps located on either side led up to the destination. As the evening progressed and more alcohol was consumed, frequent bathroom trips were necessary — not by the band, but rather by the patrons.

I don't know if it was forgetfulness or intoxication, but for some reason closing the restroom doors stopped being important. From our vantage point on stage, you couldn't quite get a full view of the inside of the facility, but you couldn't miss those coming and going. Mind you, no one intended to stare, but the scene could hardly be avoided. It was like watching a train wreck — it's awful, but for some reason you are unable to stop looking. Some women were adjusting garments as they emerged, and some were simply trying to find theirs. Many lingered on the balcony too long, trying to catch the attention of someone on the dance floor below. What a view!

We played a private party for a local industry. It was their summer employee picnic, only it was held indoors. There was no real stage, so we set up at the far end of the room. There was plenty of food and plenty of alcohol. It was a hot summer afternoon and much liquid had been consumed. At one point several women jumped up on the tables and began dancing. I use that term "dancing" loosely. Again, what a view I had!

Battle of the Bands

O N A TAMER NOTE, ONE INCARNATION OF OUR band entered a "Battle of the Bands" competition in Martinsburg. Competitions were very popular at the time. You couldn't be a professional group, whatever that meant. We had played professionally for some time so we simply decided to change the name of the band. The competition lasted two nights. I can't recall how many groups were there on the first night, but two were selected to come back on the second night, when a winner would be announced.

We were one of the two groups selected to return. We played our set and were selected as the winners. It wasn't a big prize, but it *was* money. When I went over to accept the prize, the lady in charge handed me the money and said she didn't think we were the best. I couldn't have cared less what she thought. We were from Hedgesville and our competitor was from Martinsburg. I have always thought she was just prejudiced. We divided the money among the band members, bought some refreshments, and headed for the drive-in.

GULA'S PILL

OVER THE COURSE OF OUR BAND'S HISTORY, there was a time when it was a trio. The trio was composed of Scott on drums, me on guitar, and my girlfriend, Gula, on organ — and not a compact organ or keyboard, but the full-sized, Baldwin variety. I believe our band's name was "OPUS 3." Before Gula's first public performance with the band, she got a little nervous. To ease her nervousness her mother decided to give her just half of a low-dose nerve pill. She thought that half of a pill would be the perfect amount to take the edge off.

Well, one-half of a pill was one-half too much for my very petite and sensitive girlfriend. In the middle of a song I noticed that she had stopped playing, which is easy to figure out when there are only three people in your band. The pill had relaxed her so much that she was practically immobilized. It was tough continuing with only drums and guitar, so we took a break. We escorted Gula outside for a bit and she recovered to the point that we could continue. After this incident, Gula avoided not only mystery pills from her mother, but any over-the-counter remedy that could — and in her case *would* — cause drowsiness.

THE CHIAVE CLUB

THE CHIAVE CLUB WAS A RATHER WILD SPOT. I played there while in college, toward the end of my musical heyday. This club was open very late and had a reputation which it lived up to very well. This was the club where those making the circuit on a Saturday night would end up. They began sober early in the evening, and arrived at the Chiave in the wee hours of the morning in a very different state.

I had become a member of an established local band that had surely seen its share of members come and go. In the world of rock-and-roll bands in the '60s, musicians were like spark plugs — very interchangeable and easily replaced. Our band was called "The Rejects," and it was managed by a man named Larry, who would later become my brother-in-law. We were sometimes booked to play at the Chiave until two o'clock in the morning, and we sometimes played much later than that.

My parents had shown little concern about my various musical venues until they discovered the band I was a member of was playing at the Chiave Club. Regardless, they appeared to trust my judgement and didn't interfere.

The pay was pretty good and if we were asked to remain and play after closing time, the pay got better.

Patrons arrived there inebriated and so did some of our band members. On one occasion the organ player arrived, having already begun to get his buzz on for the evening. He continued drinking between songs, and at some point during the performance his blood alcohol level hit critical mass. Suddenly, the organ dropped out of our musical equation (similar situation, different band) as its player made the short descent from the stage to the dance floor below. Our semi-conscious organ player was helped to a booth near the stage where he slept away the rest of the evening. We were able to continue however — we weren't a trio on this occasion — and played songs that were not too dependent upon the organ. I even became the organ player for a short time.

We left our instruments overnight, and upon returning the next morning to pick them up, we were met by locked doors. This wasn't too unusual, and some pounding and yelling usually got results, but not this time. After a couple of phone calls, we found out that the club's manager was being detained by local law enforcement. Our band manager helped get him released and we were able to get access to the club. All of our equipment, including a full-size organ, amplifiers, and public address system, was loaded into the 1955 Pontiac ambulance we were using for transport. The siren was gone, but it still had the lights.

I believe this was my last performance with The Rejects and my last performance at the Chiave. The club, however, did not lose it's appeal to my future brother-in-law. As I mentioned earlier, it had a reputation, and not only for its late hours and tipsy patrons. The Chiave was also known for some unsavory activities that took place there. In addition to the bar and dance floor, there were other areas where patrons could "hang out." In one such area, card games were played, and I don't mean Old Maid or bridge. These games involved money.

On one occasion, Larry became involved in one of those tempting games. At the time he was not only my future brother-in-law and manager of The Rejects, but also owned a used car lot that — in the middle of the card game — caught on fire. One of the city firemen knew where he was and phoned him at the club, informing him of the fire. Larry's hand was so good at that moment that he chose to stay in the game. I don't know if he won anything, but he lost the entire car lot to the fire.

PART FOUR

THE WORLD OF WORK

My First Paying Job

C AN YOU REMEMBER YOUR FIRST PAYING JOB? I don't mean the one a relative or family friend paid you to do. I'm talking about the one where you had to complete a task for someone who expected you to do it correctly and completely.

For me, it was shoveling snow from the sidewalks around the Methodist church in Hedgesville. This was a paying job, but not really a regular job. As soon as it stopped snowing, I now had a responsibility other than sled riding. The snow wasn't too difficult to remove, but ice could be quite a challenge. This job had not one, but *many* bosses. As this was the church I attended, it had to be done correctly or I would hear about it on Sunday morning.

—∞∞∞—

ORCHARDS AND FARMS

MY FIRST REGULAR JOB WAS IN THE ORCHARD. Not being small was to my advantage. Most orchard jobs involved moving a large wooden ladder from tree to tree. Cherries were picked for several weeks in the spring and apples were harvested in the early fall. Ground apples were picked in late fall. These jobs had a limited time frame and also came with a variety of bosses. Each orchard had its own set of rules to which you adhered.

In the summer there was hay to be made. We knew when it was time to ask various farmers if they needed help. Most were eager to hire you. One farmer who I worked for had a specific plan as to how we would do things. There was a better way, but we were not allowed to try it.

This farmer would never get off of his tractor. It was not only his working platform but was also his pulpit for imparting instruction. When bailing hay, he would drive along, pulling the wagon until it was full. We pulled up to the barn where sat a conveyor for lifting hay bales into the loft. For reasons beyond my understanding, we never used it. Instead, several of us would pass the bales to each other bucket-brigade style, until they reached the hayloft.

If you were the last person in line, you were in the top of the barn where it was the hottest and dustiest. No air ever seemed to be moving. If you stopped to look around, you could see that the air was filled with floating debris which you were, of course, inhaling. Straw was handled in a similar manner. The big difference between hay and straw is that hay could be rather soft, but not so for straw. A long-sleeve shirt would provide some protection from the sharp straw, but you would also get quite hot. A short-sleeve shirt would keep you cooler, but by the end of the day your exposed arms would look as if a crazed porcupine had attacked you.

The fields were very hot and dusty with zero shade. The farmer kept a water jug on the tractor and prided himself on letting us know when we were thirsty. This was kind of like a chain gang scenario, only without the chains.

He would also hire us to gather rocks from the fields. His position was again on the tractor, pulling behind a flatbed wagon. We were to walk along either side picking rocks from the ground and tossing them onto the wagon. This was not only hot but also terribly boring.

A migrant labor camp was located on his farm. He had an orchard and it was common for housing to be provided for the apple pickers while they worked there. It wasn't just a camp of men, but rather of entire families who would travel around from orchard to orchard picking apples. I picked several orchards but not his. The conditions under which these workers lived were not very good. Basically, they were guaranteed they would be dry and warm, and providing them with that warmth was a part of my job. I trimmed apple trees and delivered piles of firewood to the building in which they stayed.

I have saved one fact for last: our pay. No matter what task we performed, our salary was sixty cents an hour. This was the mid '60s and wages were generally low, but sixty cents and little water couldn't get you very far.

DIGGING A SEWER LINE

ONE DECEMBER A FRIEND AND I TOOK A JOB digging a sewer line for a home under construction. We were both taking part in a live Nativity scene later in the day, so we had time to do the work. The ground was frozen and we dug the trench with pick and shovel. We must have done an okay job as the same couple still lives in the house. We also looked more the part in our Nativity roles later that evening, as the dirt which covered us made us appear even more convincing as shepherds coming straight from their posts in the field to marvel at Baby Jesus. Win–win.

⸺⸙⸺

CASEY'S AUCTION

AN AUCTION IS WHAT THE BUSINESS ULTIMATELY became, but at the beginning it was just a shop that sold anything and everything. This store was located in Hedgesville at the intersection of Routes 9 and 901 in what had once been a pool hall. The building was poorly lit and smelled of stale, dirty merchandise consisting of a few new items, but mostly used ones that barely worked.

A man who went by the name of Casey Jones ran the operation, though his first name wasn't Casey. Walking inside the store required great caution. Items were stacked everywhere, and the higher the stack, the less stable it was. There was no order to anything. His most recent acquisitions were most visible while older ones became more hidden. Somehow he knew where most things were located.

His inventory came from wherever it could be purchased cheaply. A business existed in Manassas, Virginia, which sold off inventories from storage facilities and shipping companies. This is where I entered the equation: Casey needed grunt labor, and I could lift heavy objects and drive a truck. Early on Saturday mornings we would set out for Manassas in his rickety truck to buy whatever was available. Upon arriving at the warehouse all I could see were cardboard barrels with sealed lids. I wasn't privy to the negotiations, but after a few minutes he stopped talking to the owner and I began loading. He never told me if he knew the contents of those barrels or if it was a grab-bag affair.

We usually filled the truck and began our return trip by sunrise. Since it was early in the morning and we had not yet eaten breakfast, we would stop at a diner. The first time we did this, I sat with him at the counter and the waitress poured us both a cup of coffee. He added sugar and cream and I just stared at mine. I took one sip and put it back on the counter. Our greasy meals arrived and he had his cup refilled. Mine was still 99.9 percent full. After a while he noticed this fact and asked me what was wrong. I explained that I had never tasted coffee before, and that after my first taste today, I'd never order it again. Still to this day I've not had another sip of that awful-tasting dark liquid.

Casey moved his operation to Martinsburg where it became more successful. Sometimes I would stop by and we would reminisce. His sons eventually took over the business but it ultimately closed, and the buildings in Hedgesville and Martinsburg were both torn down.

SLEEPY CREEK

THERE NEVER SEEMED TO BE ANY DIFFICULTY finding a job. Almost all of them were what we call "grunt" jobs requiring more brawn than brain. My first job of any length was working at Sleepy Creek Public Area. It lasted all summer. It was hot, buggy, and snake infested but was a wonderful experience. When the summer was over, so was this job.

PURE GAS STATION

A PURE GAS STATION WAS LOCATED JUST OUTSIDE of town. I got a job there pumping gas and doing minor repairs. For a kid with a piece-of-junk car, this was a convenient place to work. My car was always in need of repair, and I was working in a garage — a perfect match.

There was a group of regulars who stopped by just to discuss current events, but most patrons came because they needed gas, oil, or repairs. The most common services were engine maintenance and tire repair. It seemed that everyone got the last mile out of every tire they owned. The garage had a steady flow of flat tires and it was rare to not have a pile of them waiting to be fixed. Tubes were still in fashion, but plugs were available for tubeless tires.

At one point the owner got into some financial trouble, and it was easy to see how this could happen. We had no cash register, but used a cigar box that wasn't locked up at night; rather, it was put under boxes of ice cream in the freezer. Anyone hanging around in the garage knew the hiding place. We had a guard dog that was let loose to roam the garage when it was closed. It was a German shepherd and looked very menacing.

Arriving for work on a Saturday morning, I quickly saw that things weren't at all the way they were supposed to be. A side window had been broken out and upon entering the garage I noticed that there were wrappers on the floor that had once contained meat. There was also no greeting from the dog. The robbers had broken the window, pitched in some wrapped meat, and with the dog appeased were able to tie him to the wall. They stole the cigar box of cash and some smokes. It wasn't an inside job, but somebody knew what they were doing.

This was but one of the factors causing the business to flounder. The owner finally got to the place where he was unable to pay me at the end of the week. He promised to do so the next, but "next week" never seemed to come. This was my first experience in financial loss, which incidentally taught me why there's a "promise" in *promissory* note.

ERNIE

WHILE WORKING AT THE PURE GAS STATION I met a man who could neither read nor write. I mean — not at all. He didn't have a car or need to be at the garage for anything auto related. He was a hard worker at a local orchard and always had a smile on his face. His tongue usually protruded from his mouth a little, making him almost impossible to understand, but we developed a language of head nods and gestures.

His reason for stopping at the station was to cash his check. The garage did sell items such as milk, bread, pop, ice cream, and tobacco products — much like convenience stores do today — but it didn't have an active check-cashing operation. This seemed to be a special service reserved just for Ernie. He would present his check to me and if I had enough money in the till, I'd cash it for him. Being unable to write, Ernie could not sign his name on the back of the check. Instead, he would scratch a squiggly-looking "$\mathcal{X}$" and I would sign my name below it. I always wondered if he even knew how much money was due to him. As I counted it out to him, he never looked at the money in his hand, but instead just stared at my face and smiled. He must have felt safe with our arrangement. Ernie seemed like such an easy target, but things were very different then.

<hr>

DODGE THE TIRE IRON

ALONG WITH TYPICAL PASSENGER AUTOMOBILES, we took care of large truck tires at the Pure gas station such as those used on pulpwood haulers and honey dippers. Our wide range of products and services meant a varied cast of customers — one of whom presented me with quite a scare one day.

We are told today not to drink and drive. I would like to add that one shouldn't drink, drive a truck with a flat tire to the garage, and continue drinking during its repair. One customer had not heeded that advice, and drove in a flat, split-rim wheel requiring some caution and strength to disassemble. It had to be done by hand as no tire changer could be used. I removed the wheel from the truck and began to take it apart on the garage floor. The inebriated truck owner just hung around the garage and continued drinking as I worked. He never stopped talking, but kept repeating that I was his buddy. I understood less and less as his words became more and more slurred.

I was listening to his ramblings while I was down on the floor, bent over, working on the wheel. Had I looked up I would have noticed what was in his hand. He had picked up the pipe from the tire changer, which is about four-feet long and about an inch-and-a-half wide. It worked well for removing tires from wheels, but that was not his intention.

I turned my head just in time to see him swing it at me. I ducked and he smiled. He continued to smile as I stood up and backed away, and he kept asking me if I was still his buddy. If he had done this only once, it might have looked like a joke, but his repeated swings made it a threat.

He was a fighter and I didn't want to go down that road, so I decided to call his home. One of his sons answered and I explained to him what was happening. A few minutes later, two of his sons arrived and tried to convince their dad to leave. He wanted no part of that.

They gently tried to pull him toward the door. He resisted and they tried to drag him out of the garage. He fought them. With both sons holding his arms down, they pushed him out of the building while he resisted every step. At this point he wasn't smiling at all but rather yelling and calling them anything but human beings.

He was finally shoved into a car and driven home. I finished fixing the tire and one of the sons returned later to drive the truck home. When the tire owner came into the garage a few days later, we talked and he didn't mention anything about the event. I don't think he remembered it at all. He paid his bill, patted me on the back, and asked, "You're my buddy, aren't you?"

DAIRY QUEEN MISTAKES

IT'S BEEN SAID THAT ONE MAN'S TRASH IS ANOTHER man's treasure, and it's sometimes true. You could buy a half-gallon of vanilla, chocolate, or Neapolitan ice cream at Poisal's store in Hedgesville. You could also purchase pre-packaged novelties such as ice cream sandwiches and anything that could be frozen on a stick. Grace's sold many of the same, and offered it by the cone. Her brand was

Breyer's, which contained dark specks of ground vanilla bean. To me it seemed odd to find black objects in a vanilla product. It tasted good but looked too much like my father's mashed potatoes after he covered them with pepper.

Dairy Queen was located in Martinsburg. I only recall going there a few times as a child. One of the managers of the store was Blanche, who lived a few miles beyond Hedgesville. It was while working at the Pure gas station that I became the lucky recipient of what would have been trash. The "trash" was the Dairy Queen mistakes of the day.

Blanche would stop by the station in the evening on her way home from work. She usually brought with her a bag or two filled with goodies that customers had decided they didn't want after ordering them. They hadn't been touched, but were simply a result of a change of mind after the preparation process had begun. These items could have just been tossed into the trash, but Blanche put them in the freezer until she left work.

After getting her car filled up, she would pay and in addition hand me a bag of delicious mistakes. Being all mixed up together, it was sometimes a challenge to figure out what some of the orders had originally been. The contents of the bag were shared with anyone who happened to be hanging around or working at the garage. We didn't really care what exactly we were eating. It was delicious and really hit the spot on a hot evening. The only problem was knowing when to stop eating, since everything had to be tasted. Too much ice cream can be a bad thing, but Blanche's sweetness has never been forgotten some fifty years later.

∞∞∞

PLEATEX

THE SUMMER BEFORE ENTERING COLLEGE, I GOT a job in the garment industry, such as it was. I like the way that sounds, but it actually was just a sweatshop in the truest sense of the word. It was one of the last vestiges of the old Interwoven Mill complex in Martinsburg. This kid from Hedgesville was truly out of his element in this work environment. I was accustomed to working outside in nature. There was nothing natural about this place at all.

This was, without a doubt, the worst job I ever had in my life up to this point. In retrospect I can safely say it was *the worst job I ever had in my entire life.* The person in charge of this hellhole could not have cared less about you as an individual. He wanted product — and only product — from you.

The factory was located on the basement level of a building with no windows or ventilation. Let me reiterate: there were absolutely no windows or anything connecting you to the outside, except the entry door from the street. As the name so cleverly reveals, this factory put pleats into fabric that eventually became skirts and dresses. You and your partner worked on opposite sides of a long table. First you unrolled and clamped down an accordion-folded, cardboard pattern. Next you rubbed wax on the pattern to create a slightly tacky surface. Then you unrolled cloth from a large bolt of material located at the bottom end of the table, placing it appropriately into the crevices of the pattern. When the pattern was completed, you cut the fabric free from the bolt, then carefully gathered the prepared fabric, tied it, and placed it in a cart.

Once the cart was full it was removed and rolled with others into an oven-like chamber. The doors closed and the prepared fabric was heated and infused with a chemical mixture containing formaldehyde to permanently set the pleats. From there I don't know where it went. My job was simply to imprint the pattern correctly to the cloth, which I must have done okay, as I advanced from solids to plaids that required a degree of skill in alignment and matching.

The workplace was hot and distinctively smelly from chemicals utilized in the pleat-making process. If you don't know, formaldehyde is a volatile organic compound with various industrial applications. It's more commonly known as embalming fluid, and is *now* a known carcinogen. OSHA would have had a field day. We were given a short break in the morning and in the afternoon a roach coach awaited us for snacks. I don't know how anyone could eat. My stomach was in a perpetual state of queasiness from the fumes. Pay was a dollar per hour. The manager made sure you never worked beyond forty hours a week or else he'd have to pay an extra twenty-five cents for those hours.

In addition to my pay I also received a free education. There is no polite way to explain what went on at this factory. Many of the women were absolutely vulgar and crude. In an adjoining room, bolts of material were stored and some sewing took place. Several of the female workers had their own business going on in there. You might say it was the oldest known female profession. I only assume it was a business. Maybe no money was exchanged.

In addition to these comings and goings, there were words and phrases used that I had only heard men use at local watering holes. On top of this were the wax creations, and I don't mean the kind that would be on display at a wax museum. The large blocks of wax we used to rub onto the patterns to make them tacky were molded into anatomically correct male body parts and were presented like trophies to some of the other women. I don't know what happened to them after that.

Any of the above-mentioned things would result in a lawsuit today, but back then they were taken in stride. Have I mentioned how terrible it was to work there? I know I have, but I can't emphasize it enough. The only positive thing about this job was that I eventually made enough money to pay for my first semester of college. This job taught me that I needed to get an education because this wasn't something I wanted to have to do for very long.

Mr. 15

I N THE FALL OF 1966 I WAS LOOKING FOR A JOB to pay for my second semester of college. Along came Mr. 15. Before the local invasion of fast-food franchises, one local businessman decided to open his own version of a fast-food restaurant. It was called Mr. 15 because everything in it cost just fifteen cents.

I was hired and was part of the grand opening. The restaurant served the traditional array of burgers and fries, but also offered fried chicken — not processed chicken, but real chicken parts. The only problem with this was that the business had minimal refrigeration — a fact either overlooked or intentionally omitted by the owner.

The lack of refrigeration seemed to me like a rather big problem, but the owner didn't think so. Trash bags were cut open and placed on the floor. Cardboard boxes were configured into a square and stacked high to form walls. The bags were placed over the boxes, chicken was dumped in, and ice was scattered on top to cover the chicken — instant refrigeration. As the ice melted, you just added more. The cold, bloody meltwater seepage conveniently found its way to the nearest floor drain. Occasionally we would fish out the chicken parts and rotate the inventory. The chicken on the bottom would be bleached out and look just awful, but it was cooked and served.

When I got out of class at Shepherd, I headed straight to Mr. 15. Cooking was done on a flat top and a fryer. It could have been the perfect job to gain weight, but was just the opposite. I lost weight because the food was really bad and the constant smell of grease and oil diminished my appetite.

My brain was telling my body I was full due to the smell, but my body thought differently.

This was the only job in my life that I ever quit. The owner even tried to entice me into quitting college and working for him full time. He was going to franchise this operation. None of this ever happened. The hours were a killer. I would work until one o'clock in the morning, clean the place up, drive home, and arrive at about two o'clock in the morning. I would then clean myself up and study for a while. Sleep consisted of a couple of hours because I was back on the road at a quarter past seven, headed to college. I don't think anyone could keep up that schedule for long. I decided to quit Mr. 15 and begin searching for another way to finance my sophomore year of college.

WEST VIRGINIA DEPARTMENT OF HIGHWAYS

SUMMER WAS ALMOST HERE AND I FOUND A JOB with the West Virginia Department of Highways (DOH). Part of my time was spent with two men, traveling the back roads of the county and patching potholes. I saw a lot of back roads and a lot of potholes.

These two older gentlemen acted like a married couple. They must have worked together for a long time. To me it was just a hole in the road requiring asphalt, but to them it was an art — each pothole was unique and required observation and careful planning. The perimeter had to be just so and all debris removed from within. An appropriate amount of asphalt was placed into the hole and then the rear wheels of the truck were run back and forth over the patch until it met their exacting standards. I viewed patches differently after this experience.

Another part of the job was working along Interstate 81. I was part of a crew that walked the entire length of it in West Virginia — all twenty-six miles of it — scraping and sanding guardrails. We walked the northbound lanes from the Virginia line to the Maryland line, then headed back to the Virginia line, completing the southbound lanes. When this task was finished, we walked the distances again, this time painting the guardrails — *with brushes.* (The DOH had a machine to spray paint the guardrails but they didn't allow us to use it for fear we'd paint a passing car.) Finally we were each given a mowing scythe and were sent off on another round-trip excursion to cut thistle along the shoulder of the road.

This job was not supervised. We were simply dropped off in the morning and collected in the evening. There were very few spots to get any shade, and sudden downpours would find us — if we were lucky — taking shelter in the large drainpipes under the interstate. I can only imagine what the passing motorists thought when they saw us workers — perpetually drenched from either sweat or rain. But the highway looked great! This progressive roadside beautification assignment ultimately required walking the distance between two states six times, and in doing so traversing about 156 miles on foot.

C.L.'S GARAGE

MY FUTURE FATHER-IN-LAW WAS KIND ENOUGH to also provide me with employment. I had enough experience working at a garage to help him out with repairs on weekends, but I've always attributed my employment there to being his daughter's boyfriend. "C.L." was a nickname I gave him after Gula and I were married. Carl was a fabulous mechanic and operated his repair business in Martinsburg. He was also a true mechanic having been trained by General Motors with a specialty in transmissions.

In the early '50s he worked at Dailey Motors and Charlie Brooks, both of which were GM dealerships.

Later he owned a full-service Amoco gas station. At the time I helped him he strictly performed repairs. He could replace a Corvair engine in a couple of hours. He worked on cars from 1930s to 1960s models. There were always cars there in various stages of repair. He amazed me with his ability to diagnose the problem with nothing but a large screwdriver and a length of heater hose.

After repairing an automatic transmission he would lay on a creeper and the transmission would be placed on top of him. With his knees bent, the yoke would be placed on his legs and the bell housing on his arms. He would then slide under the car, which wasn't on a lift but rather sitting on supports only a foot or two off the floor. Using nothing but himself for leverage, he would slide the transmission into place holding it with only his legs, and begin replacing the bolts to secure it in place.

One thing he couldn't do was say "no" to a customer. If someone showed up with a problem, he wouldn't hesitate to stop what he was doing and look at their car. He would freely extend credit to customers, fixing their cars with the understanding they would pay him in the future. Some customers didn't always live up to their end of the bargain, but some did, and in quite peculiar ways. One woman, for instance, paid the entire repair bill for her 1930-something Plymouth in coins — silver fifty-cent pieces. I asked him to pay me with them. He did and I still have them today.

He did have one bad habit: when he put a tool down, he had trouble finding it again. He solved this problem by buying more tools from the salespeople who traveled to garages each week. Eventually, when he closed the business, I helped clean things up. On the floor, under several inches of absorbent granules, we recovered most of his lost wrenches. There must have been seventy-five, half-inch, ⁹⁄₁₆ wrenches both open and boxed end. I also still have a few of them today. Unfortunately neither my tools nor my skills get much use these days, as I can barely navigate beneath the hood of a vehicle built after 1980.

NICHOLS

I HEARD THAT A NEW STORE HAD RECENTLY OPENED up in Martinsburg and was looking for help. Before the days of Walmart and Target there was Nichols Discount City. It was the biggest store that had ever come to

Martinsburg. It was the size of a present-day Kmart and carried just about the same types of products. Since there had never been anything like it in town before, it was the place to go. I decided to apply for a part-time job.

My interview went well and I was hired to work in the sporting goods department, where I felt right at home. There was a store manager, two assistant managers, and many department heads in addition to "grunts" like me. The store was open from ten o'clock in the morning to ten o'clock at night, Monday through Saturday, and noon to six o'clock in the evening on Sunday. Since I was back at school, ten o'clock was a much better closing time than that of the establishment I worked at my freshman year of college, and I was able to get a couple more hours of sleep.

The obnoxious store manager — and I mean that in the nicest way — would yell at you and question everything you did. He was a man of very heavy stature, and usually had a cigar in his mouth. He had come here from the New York metropolitan area and I'm not sure how he felt about us rather rural folks. It didn't take me long to figure out that to get along with him you must try to make yourself invisible. Regardless, this job seemed like one I should latch onto and ride out until I graduated from college. It was indoors, air-conditioned, and didn't involve the dangers of walking the highway or being exposed to toxic chemical vapors.

A year or so into this job, the manager walked past the sporting goods department one evening. He stopped, looked at me, and yelled, "Engle! What have we got here, an (expletive) roadblock?" We were in the process of removing summer items from the shelves and replacing them with winter items. The aisles were truly packed. I arrived at work that evening and inherited the mess from the day shift. The manager confronted me about it several times that evening, but I just wasn't able to complete the seasonal changeover during my shift. He didn't appear to be too happy about it, and I feared this might be the end of my employment.

Some time passed and I thought everything was cool. Then one evening the manager approached me and as he often did, yelled, "Engle!" I didn't know what to expect when he began talking, but I soon was quite surprised. He asked me if I would like to train for an assistant manager's position. Of course I agreed.

Nothing happened right away, but sometime later, while at Shepherd College, a message was delivered from the administration office. It was from the store manager of Nichols telling me to be there within the hour. I left class, broke the speed limit, and arrived to find the manager and several other New York big wigs waiting for me. It was another interview. I passed their test and a few months later became an assistant-manager-in-training. I was in charge of four departments: sporting goods, hardware, seasonal, and notions — with all those spools of thread, buttons, snaps, and bolts of fabric. Now, those I had been working alongside of referred to me as their boss.

PUNCHING BOXES

THERE WAS A TREMENDOUS AMOUNT OF WORK TO do in my new position at Nichols, and rarely could I just stand around. I had to keep an eye on anything that went wrong and could eventually become my problem. I always had to be thinking ahead, and planning for the upcoming seasons. It always felt a little strange to be ordering Christmas ornaments in the heat of summer.

Part of my upgraded duties was to arrange seasonal displays in the center of the store, and on one occasion I was helping create one for summer. I didn't have my box cutter with me so I was using a closed fist to smash the tops of boxes and open them. This was a technique I had successfully employed many times before. This time, however, after punching a box and pulling my hand back out, the box came with it. There was a very warm feeling in my hand. I pulled the box away and was greeted by blood pulsing from the holes in my hand. I attempted to stop the squirting blood but it wasn't working. In fact, it was shooting out far enough to hit the side of a swimming pool that was on display.

I tried first to stop the bleeding by holding tightly to my wounded hand with my other hand, but it wasn't working. I then headed to the office and then directly to the hospital. Doctors there were able to stop the bleeding. I returned to the store and followed my own trail of blood back to the scene of the crime, curious to see what had caused this fiasco. I picked up the bloody box and, upon opening it correctly, discovered it was full of rotisserie skewers pointing upright. The sharp metal spikes were now tipped with red — *my* red. From that time on I always remembered to carry a box cutter.

THE GREAT NICHOLS ROBBERY

THE NICHOLS DEPARTMENT STORE BUILDING HAD an adjoining Grand Union grocery store on its north side. A large metal pull-down gate separated the two stores. When the stores were open, the gate was rolled up to the ceiling and the stores appeared to be one, though they were two separate businesses. The grocery store's main office — including its safe — was visible to the public. Not so for Nichols. The public could see only the front of the Nichols office complex. Windows on both sides of the main office were used for refunds and layaways. What the public could not see was the manager's office, counting room, and safe.

Some criminals decided to rob both stores in the wee hours of the morning. They thought they had it all figured out. Our store was alarmed with both loud bells on site and a direct link to the police department. The burglars didn't enter Nichols directly, but luckily for them, broke into the grocery store which had no working alarm system.

Some train tracks ran directly behind the stores. Across the tracks toward the west was a construction site with heavy equipment, including a truck with a winch and metal cable. The thieves entered the construction site, took the end of the cable with them, and crossed the tracks to the store. They entered the building through a door on the grocery side, dragging the cable with them. Having cased the place beforehand, the robbers knew exactly where the safe was located in the grocery store office, so they simply wrapped the cable around it and pulled it out of the store.

The store had a huge pyramid display of ketchup at least five feet tall. It was between the office and the point of entry for the robbers. When they engaged the winch and began pulling the safe, its trajectory was straight to the door, right through the ketchup display. When the pyramid toppled, the bottles fell and burst on the floor, leaving shards of glass among pools of red. The safe was pulled out of the store, leaving red streaks of ketchup in its wake.

After removing the grocery safe, they cut through the metal gate and entered Nichols. Unable to get to the Nichols safe, they headed for the sporting goods section, stopping first to get several large trash cans. They broke into the locked cabinets housing firearms and threw them into the cans.

Their task complete, they left the store. Instead of going out the same door they had entered, they exited a door near the shoe department. This was their fatal flaw. They weren't expecting the loud alarm bells to ring, as the robbers had climbed onto the roof beforehand and filled the bells with salt, rendering them mute. When they opened the door, it was silent indeed, but unbeknownst to the robbers, it triggered the silent alarm directly to the police station.

It wasn't uncommon for the silent alarm to sound at the police station. A storm often triggered the alarm, and in such cases one of the managers would meet the police at the front door, go inside, and reset the alarm. On this occasion, after receiving the customary call from the police department, I went to the store expecting to just reset the alarm. However, upon entering, I quickly realized that this time it was the real thing. In fact, it looked like the scene of a massacre. The police had arrived there fast enough to actually prevent the completion of the robbery. They didn't catch the thieves, but recovered the merchandise. The guns were taken to the police barracks as evidence. I brought in the paperwork to identify each of them by serial number, but we didn't get the firearms back before I left the job.

One little mishap by the crooks undermined what would have been a rather ambitious, creative, and perfectly orchestrated robbery. Of all folks, you'd expect robbers as bold as these to remember: the devil's in the details.

STICKY FINGERS

RETAIL WAS NEVER BORING, AND THE PUBLIC made sure of it through the art of shoplifting. Nichols had security guards in uniform and some in plain clothes. By observing a spectrum of techniques from the subtle to the obvious, I got an education in the art of stealing. Some people just saw something they couldn't resist. For them it wasn't a matter of real need, and it was hard to feel sympathy when they got caught. Other cases were sad. A young girl stealing lipstick was one thing, but a young woman stealing formula for her baby was another. There were even families of both adults and children who would swarm the place and work as a team. The one and only constant thing I had to remember was — it was *all* stealing.

There was one family who didn't steal directly but had a method of using the system to their advantage. They devised a way to have their cake and eat it too. In early spring they would purchase fishing equipment for their entire family, including adults and children alike. When September arrived, they would come to the refund desk with the fishing gear and ask for a refund. They told us something was wrong with all of it. Our return policy was very lenient and all of their money was refunded. They would then head directly to the shoe and clothing departments and purchase school clothes. The clothing was never returned, but the family managed to eat and be clothed with the same money. Perhaps this was the rather nefarious precursor to the popular marketing trend of "buy one, get one free."

<hr />

KEEPING US HONEST

THEFT PREVENTION WAS A BIG CONCERN FOR Nichols. Major heists were handled by local law enforcement. Customers with sticky fingers were handled by security guards. But stealing was also an inside job, and neither management nor staff were exempt from discovery and eventual dismissal.

Standing in the office one afternoon, looking over some paperwork, a man I had never seen before came to the window and asked me to hand him the manager's coat. I did so and shortly thereafter watched as the manager was escorted from the store. He was gone and never to return. There had been a promotion going on in the appliance department and anyone purchasing a large appliance was to receive a coupon for a free turkey. Turns out the manager had kept the coupons and was giving them to his friends. He was also pocketing expensive cigars from the smoke shop. I can't imagine having to explain losing your upper management position over some turkeys and cigars!

Monitoring middle management and store employees was not left to a chance observation of indiscretion. Enter the polygraph, or more commonly known as the lie detector test. An outside company was hired to come into the store unannounced and administer the polygraph on selected employees. If you have never had that experience, it can be a little unnerving. I won't go into specifics, but the general idea of the test is to make you cleanse your soul. The examiner first asked some general questions to establish a baseline, and then moved on to more specific questions about taking or giving away anything belonging to the company and so on.

Once the test was complete, employees were excused from the room without knowing whether they had passed or failed. Managers, however, immediately got the results and were told to take action — a part of the job I never liked. Shortly after an employee failed the test, I had to inform them they were being terminated, using any other reason than the fact they'd failed the polygraph. The tests were more frequent for middle managers, but my honesty and even temper never failed me.

Things went well at work for quite some time, and upon graduation from college and receiving my teaching degree, I stayed with the company. My time at Nichols was enjoyable and they treated my wife and me very well. I had actually considered staying with the company and not teaching, but that would have required making a big move out of the area. A position had opened near Richmond, Virginia, and I was in line to take it. We chose to remain close to our families. I left Nichols in the summer of 1971 only after accepting a teaching position in Hagerstown, Maryland. The time had come to try out this teaching thing.

PART FIVE

COLLEGE BOUND

Four Years of Change

I WAS NOW EIGHTEEN YEARS OLD, AND EACH OF those years had been spent living in my little world in and around Hedgesville. Music had allowed me to experience things beyond the town and had even taken me to New York City, but my steady point of reference was Hedgesville, and all of the experiences I had collected from my childhood there.

Everything was about to change. The last days of high school were passing quickly and deadlines lay ahead. That wonderful feeling one has at the end of the school year wasn't there. Instead, I was feeling overwhelmed and afraid. Decisions had to be made and each of them came with consequences. It was up to me to decide what I was going to do with the rest of my life.

I couldn't begin to imagine what was ahead for me. So many changes would be taking place and many of them were out of the realm of my control. Family life had taught me what it meant to care for and support loved ones. My schooling had given me as much "book learning" as it could. Living in the country had given me skills such as hunting, fishing, camping and being independent. Various jobs had taught me responsibility. All of these factors would help prepare me for what was to come as my rather simple, protected world expanded in many directions.

It is said that the journey of 1,000 miles begins with a single step. Taking that first step after high school graduation was the beginning of a life-long journey.

COLLEGE PREP

IN THE SPRING OF 1966, AS A HIGH SCHOOL SENIOR, it was time to make some important decisions about my future. The cocoon of high school was about to dissolve and a plan was needed for future endeavors. Whether I thought I was ready or not, some choices had to be made.

High school had been so much fun. There hadn't been a need to plan too far ahead. After graduation it was expected that I would know with certainty what my future would hold. If circumstances had been different, I probably would have been happy taking a regular day job and using the evenings and weekends to play music. But given the time in which I was living, that plan just wouldn't work.

World events had now begun to influence even the little town of Hedgesville. The draft was now in effect, and the likelihood of being called for military service after graduation was almost certain. You could not escape this fact unless you skipped out of the country. That was never a thought, and I just assumed my time to serve would come.

If you attended college you could receive a deferment, which meant you wouldn't be called to military service until after graduation. Taking into account the footage I was seeing on television coming out of Southeast Asia, continuing my education seemed like a very good idea.

Attending college was a decision I had made on my own. There was no family discussion. It wasn't that my parents didn't care what I was planning. As no one in my family other than my grandmother had attended college, my parents really couldn't offer much advice. My family was representative of many of my classmates' families. Most were working class and college didn't hold the high level of importance that it does today. I never experienced the years of preparation or family discussions that dominate students' lives today as they plan their future. I'm sure my parents were proud of my choice, but it was never discussed.

It also didn't help that our senior class had received the bare minimum in college preparatory counseling. I, however, had taken the necessary academic courses to get into most colleges, including two years of foreign language. Perhaps in the back of my mind I had always known I'd further my education. When applying to college, you had to send your transcript showing you had completed the appropriate classwork and earned sufficient grades. I really had not been too concerned with grades throughout high school. I certainly could have done better but performed well enough to make the honor roll most of the time.

What I became aware of was the need to take either the ACT or SAT tests, and score high enough to be accepted at a college. The ACT exam was needed if you were going to attend an in-state college, and the SAT was required for out-of-state admission. Economics has a way of influencing some of our opportunities in life. It certainly determined where I would attend college, as the possibility of me paying for out-of-state tuition was zero. Since in-state it would be, I set my sights on nearby Shepherd College and signed up for the ACT. With little to no preparation, I took the test and luckily received a score well above what was required for admission.

Having Shepherd so close was a great thing. It had a good reputation as being a teacher's college. The student enrollment was very low — just over 1,000. It didn't matter what the emphasis of the college was because it was my only real option. I applied and was accepted. The first step to making college a reality was complete.

The next step would be figuring out how I would pay for college. The high school guidance counselor mentioned we could apply for scholarships. They were few and far between, but I applied for one. He contacted me after graduation and assured me I would be receiving one, though it wouldn't be a very large amount. Any free money sounded good to me. Weeks went by and I heard nothing. I eventually found out that the scholarship had been given to another student. That was a sharp blow to my plans. Now there would be no living on campus. I would commute as the majority of students did, and in my case that would be a drive of some twenty miles each way, every day. At least my car was in good shape so my means of transportation was covered. I would also have to keep working nights, weekends, and summers to pay for expenses.

I spent the summer before college working in a garment factory for a dollar an hour. I saved a little, at least enough to start the college enrollment process. My parents told me they would help with my expenses, but this seemed strange because they barely had enough money to get by. It ends up that the total financial assistance they provided for my entire four years of college was twenty-five dollars. Living at home certainly helped curtail expenses, but there was no more money coming in. I would be financing my education.

Envelopes began arriving in our mailbox with forms to be completed and preliminary things to be done. Among them was the required freshman reading list including books to read before classes even began. Somehow during the summer I was to squeeze in *Brave New World* and *1984*. Prior to starting college I was also to select a major. My interests had always been centered around the outdoors and playing music. When it came to choosing a major, the outdoors won. The outlined curriculum for a biology major looked good to me. The selection of courses was varied and seemed exciting. Finally, we were to prepare our four-year plan, and outline our course schedules. It seemed like a daunting task, but I charted my course. Rather than just taking science classes with no real goal, I decided I would be a teacher. That was a revelation because it had never before crossed my mind.

∞

FIRST-YEAR FRESHMAN

S HEPHERD WAS A SMALL COLLEGE IN THE '60S, and its size provided the perfect environment to meet and become lifelong friends with people I had never before seen. It is remarkable how quickly friendships formed — especially among the commuters. Those of us in the same field of study connected primarily because we saw each other in the same classes each week. Perhaps we needed that camaraderie in order to help each other in studying. It's funny, but the friends with whom I spent just four years of college became a bigger part of my life today than those with whom I spent twelve years of school.

Class sizes were small and each department had only a few professors who taught multiple courses over the years you were there. By years I mean *four* years. Very few full-time students ever considered the possibility of going an extra semester, let alone a fifth year.

I was about as green a student as you could find. I paid my ninety-seven dollar tuition — the amount required to carry a full load of classes. With book list in hand I went to the college bookstore, soon to realize that my textbooks were going to cost more than my tuition. No matter my financial situation, the last thing to be purchased was a gold and blue beanie.

The Shepherd beanie was an unwritten prerequisite for entering freshmen. If caught without it, upper classmen could ask you to perform tasks such as counting the bricks in a section of the walkway. You supposedly got demerits each time you were caught not wearing it, and if you received enough, disciplinary action would be taken. It was rumored you could even be expelled from college. I'm almost certain nothing would have happened if you refused to participate in this mild form of hazing. The whole thing seemed ridiculous to me so off came the beanie in a matter of a few days.

I was going to college with the best plan I could create. College was going to be a day job that paid nothing, and I would be moonlighting in order to pay for it. I would not have a chance to experience what I had seen on television and in the movies as the "college experience." In fact, over the course of four years I never saw a single athletic event. No football. No basketball. No baseball. Not one! They were held at night or on weekends — when I was working. There were neither fraternities nor school organizations in my sights. There just wasn't time to spare. When class was over, I jumped into my car and headed to work. I did not know it any other way. My situation wasn't unique. Other commuters were doing just about the same thing.

I'm sure those students living on campus had a totally different experience. Many didn't have to work during college to fund their education. Their out-of-class time was spent enjoying the many activities that college life provides. As I reflect on that time, I think, perhaps, that students living on campus didn't have to grow up as quickly as those who did not. They could just be more carefree. That must have been a wonderful feeling.

If you are hoping to read some crazy college stories such as those that took place in the movie *Animal House,* you are going to be disappointed. There just wasn't any time for fooling around. Studying had to be taken seriously, as failure to maintain at least a 2.0 GPA could result in the loss of a deferment. Having to live off-campus was one thing, but shipping out to Southeast Asia was quite another.

—∞∞∞—

DEAN MOLLY

E VERY STUDENT TOOK A COLLEGE ORIENTATION class called, "On Becoming an Educated Person." It was one credit hour and lasted half of the first semester. The class was located in the library basement, and had a rather large number of students. The Dean of Women, Dean Molly, taught it. She couldn't see very well and had multiple pairs of glasses attached to chains that hung from her neck. She also couldn't hear very well, so she wore a hearing aide. Its volume control was attached to the front of her clothing. Some students took great pleasure in exploiting Dean Molly's sensorial limitations.

The basement classroom had a network of support columns throughout which were used to exploit Dean Molly's limited vision. The trick was to get behind one of the large columns and say something out loud. She would respond to the question but was unable to see the student. She'd cycle between her multiple pairs of glasses, looking intently at the students. It wouldn't have mattered if she had a telescope. She would have needed Superman's X-ray vision to have located the questioner. This game ended with the person just saying nothing.

Another student took total advantage of Dean Molly's limited hearing. He would raise his hand to ask a question. When recognized by her, he would move his mouth but not utter a sound. She would strain to hear him. When that didn't work she would adjust the level of her hearing aide. He continued his silent treatment until she cranked up the hearing aide so loud it squealed. Then he would begin talking loudly or almost yelling and she would turn the volume down. The process would repeat until laughter gave away the prank.

THE RAM'S DEN

THE ONE THING I DID SHARE WITH ALL OTHER college students was the Student Union. Ours was called the Ram's Den, named after the college mascot. It was the college-sponsored lounge and eatery, a popular place for students to gather between classes. Some studying happened there, but mostly just eating and relaxing. This is where I enjoyed a diversion from both school and work by playing bridge quite regularly. Some serious internal debate took place as to whether or not a good hand should trump going to class, and a good hand sometimes did.

It was in the Ram's Den that I observed those who were having what I would call the "true college experience." They were immediately identifiable. Their appearance and actions were carefree, and they seemed — more often than not — to be in a state of extreme contentment. Many had joined fraternities and sororities and formed cliques. They were part of the college lifestyle and I was just attending classes. We both had the same ultimate goal, but I think those living on campus had a lot more fun getting there.

As commuters, we didn't have meal plans for dining in the college cafeteria. Therefore, the Ram's Den was our primary food source, and the lunch options offered were limited. Usually I lived on twenty-cent steamers and an occasional order of French fries. For a special treat I would order a forty-cent Chuck Wagon sandwich. Sometimes I would brownbag it, but not often. That required preparation at home and my time there was scarce. Some commuters who had cash-flow problems got creative with condiments. One such student wanted tomato soup and improvised with a cup of hot water and some ketchup.

There was always something happening at the Ram's Den, and it wasn't always good. On one occasion a student was running toward the building. He jumped over the patio wall to run into the Den, believing the sliding glass doors were open. They were not. He crashed into the glass and looked as if he had been mauled by a wild animal.

SLEEP STUDY

M Y PARENTS INQUIRED VERY LITTLE ABOUT MY college experience. In fact, I saw very little of them. An eight o'clock class meant leaving home no later than a quarter past seven in the morning. Returning home from work meant arriving well past midnight. Eventually I found a job that got me home by half past ten.

My father had taken a job working evening and night shifts. My mother worked during the day. Rarely did the family sit down together. Purely out of necessity, a new mode of communicating developed: The Steno Pad. It sat with a pencil on the kitchen table, and is where we wrote notes and exchanged information. Daily highlights were jotted down alongside issues needing attention. It was our primitive, analog form of group texting, and it continued past the time I moved away from home until my father got a day job. It kept communication flowing and helped us to feel connected, even when our paths rarely crossed.

Along with a lack of family time, there was little time for fun. I would study, clean up, sleep a few hours, and then head back to class. Many students pursuing other majors attended classes on Mondays, Wednesdays, and Fridays. Science classes, however, were accompanied by Tuesday and Thursday labs. Therefore, I attended college five days each week.

Finding enough time for studying was difficult. Certain classes required a great amount of study. My classmates and I would gather as a group either in the Ram's Den or at the college library for cram sessions. When that wasn't enough, we would all invade one of our homes and pull an "all nighter." Physics class involved heavy studying to learn what seemed like a zillion equations. My classmates and I reviewed them so often that we could visualize them as they appeared in our notes. Our professor told us he taught physics and not math. He cared less about if you got the right answer to a problem, and more about if you knew the correct formula and procedure to solve it. This was a good thing, as I had no calculus in high school. I taught myself from a textbook during breaks at work.

Given my particular circumstances, the issue of sleep was a tough problem to solve. There are only so many hours in a day. Sometimes my schedule would afford me a couple of hours between classes. As much as I liked playing bridge, I also liked sleeping. Many people snicker when they talk about the back seat of a car. I have fond memories of the back seat of my '62 Chevy, as it was where I slept whenever I had the chance. When parked under the large trees behind the English building, it was quite cool and comfortable. Restrooms were conveniently located on the lower level of the building, accessible directly from the parking lot. Life was good.

<hr/>

STORY OF THE MISSING HOMEWORK

WHILE ATTENDING COLLEGE, MY 1962 CHEVY was in the shop for repairs. My parents allowed me to borrow the 1959 station wagon for transportation to and from school. All the vehicles we had were either parked inside, beside, or behind the barn each evening. We never had any trouble with vandalism or theft, but we kept them locked just the same.

I returned home from work late one evening, parked behind the barn, grabbed the books I needed to study that night, and locked up the car. Early the next morning I left the house and walked the short distance up to the barn. Rounding the corner of the building, I expected to see the red and white land yacht sitting where I had docked it, but I didn't.

At first I didn't think much of it. I knew I was the last person to drive it, and the thought crossed my mind that maybe I had parked it somewhere else. Or maybe someone else was using it this morning. These explanations left my mind as quickly as they entered. I had definitely parked behind the barn last night, and I was the only one up at this ungodly hour of the morning. The reality of the situation was that the '59 wagon was gone.

I quickly made it back down the path to the house and woke my parents, telling them that the car was missing. They got up and went to the barn to see for themselves. I don't know what they thought they would see. If the car was gone a moment ago, there was little likelihood it had magically reappeared. No matter what they had expected, we all confirmed firsthand that the car was indeed missing. I then realized that it was not only the car that was gone, but also the majority of my books and papers.

Instead of attending my classes, I spent the day filing

paperwork with the state police. This just seemed like a formality to me. The car — along with my necessary college materials — was gone, and why weren't they out looking for them? In the meantime, my '62 Chevy was quickly repaired and returned into circulation, so at least I would have transportation the next day. My father had a truck, so the entire family remained mobile.

Several days passed and I returned home from college one afternoon with my father waiting for me. The '59 wagon had been recovered and was now in a repair shop in Martinsburg. It hadn't been driven to the shop, but rather towed, which sounded rather ominous. We drove to the shop and there it was. From a distance it didn't look too much the worse for its mysterious adventure.

The police were there and explained that we couldn't take the vehicle home. We could only remove items that we could prove were ours. This sounded rather strange, but under the watchful eyes of the law I retrieved the schoolbooks and assorted papers that were undoubtedly mine. Upon closer inspection I could see that the front end of the wagon was messed up. I later discovered that the transmission was messed up as well. What I found most fascinating, however, was what I observed in the roof of the car — a rather large bullet hole!

After contacting the police when we first noticed the car was AWOL, my father and I had driven around the area, playing cops, looking for the car. We had even seen some tracks toward the end of Cannon Hill and followed them all the way to where they stopped. We found no car.

Ends up we were looking for the car in all the wrong places. The car thieves had taken the car into Maryland, near Boonsboro, and robbed a gas station. The police had been alerted and apparently a high-speed chase ensued. As crazy as it sounds, the police had actually put that bullet hole in the car. I don't know if they were returning fire, but shots were fired.

The thieves ditched the car and fled the scene on foot, never to be captured and brought to justice. The repair shop kept the car a few weeks, fixed the hole and front end, and repaired the transmission. It was returned home as good as new, but now with a new distinction: getaway-car status! I was also now the proud owner of the world's greatest excuse for my homework being late, and it was so much more exciting than it having been eaten by a dog.

—◈◈◈—

Things That Go Bump in the Lab

THE MOST MEMORABLE COLLEGE EXPERIENCES I recall happened in class. In Histology class we were making slides using our own blood, which we did quite often. Most of us could carry out this exercise without event, but Dick, a classmate and friend, passed out. It was like watching something happen in slow motion. He fell forward into a low lab sink, and on his descent to the floor managed to hit his chin, nose, and forehead.

We watched and some even applauded as Dick had a habit of acting out a character from a very popular show at the time, Laugh-In. The character, Tyrone F. Horneigh, often did falls. When we saw the blood and his green skin tone, however, we knew this was not an act. Fortunately, neither Dick's face nor the lab sink suffered any permanent damage. Unfortunately — for Dick — this story gained traction and formed a lasting legacy.

—◈◈◈—

Dr. Bell: 101

ONE OF MY FAVORITE AND MOST INTERESTING professors was Dr. Bell. It can be corroborated by any of his former students that this man has an impeccable memory. His lectures were held on Mondays, Wednesdays, and Fridays. He never had notes in front of him, and when class began he would just begin lecturing. He wrote on a chalkboard and when the class ended he simply stopped. At our next class, he picked up exactly where he had left off, and continued — even if he had been in mid sentence.

Dr. Bell taught a variety of subjects and was equally knowledgeable in each of them. He dressed the same way each day in a sport coat that matched nothing else he was wearing. He had a deep voice and a devilish smile which remained his expression whether he was congratulating or correcting you. Dr. Bell was somewhat carefree in his demeanor, yet intensely serious. When talking to him it was evident he was paying full attention to what you were saying by his responses, but it also appeared that part of his mind was off on another thought.

On one occasion he entered our classroom with his sport coat covered in recently hatched preying mantises. He reached into a pocket and produced a glass vial and some tweezers. He carefully extracted several insects from his coat and placed them into the vial, handed it to a student and said, "You might like to have these."

Dr. Bell's office looked like an ecological composting experiment gone terribly wrong. Items were stacked up everywhere. Sometime after the preying mantis incident, a fellow student admitted to me that he had placed several egg cases in Dr. Bell's office, knowing they would not be detected. How Dr. Bell came to be completely covered with them I don't know, but it didn't really seem too out of character for him to be so.

My wife, Gula, was working as secretary at the time for the Division of Science and Math. She worked for all of my professors — including Dr. Bell, who never minced words and had a very dry sense of humor. She would joke with him and the other professors. Immediately outside of Gula's office was a large aquarium. On one occasion she told Dr. Bell that he should say something to the fish in the tank. As usual, he smiled and stared. She repeated her request, and he turned toward the fish tank and stated, "A big fish is going to eat you all." She told him that was not a very nice thing to say and that the comment would upset them. He looked back at the tank and said, "Perhaps he won't eat you all."

ENTOMOLOGY

E NTOMOLOGY CLASS REQUIRED EACH STUDENT to assemble a collection of insects. Finding unusual insects from as many orders as possible was the goal, so a group of us headed to the C&O Canal along the Potomac River. We came upon a campsite and the remains of some campfires. From what we *thought* we knew, the firebrat — a not-so-common insect — could be found in the ashes.

We dug into the ashes and, sure enough, there were insects that we knew just had to be firebrats. We all dug and collected — some for ourselves and extras for fellow classmates. When we returned to class, everyone wanted to take credit for our discovery, boasting, "I saw them first," "I found the most," or "I have some for everyone."

Dr. Bell just stared in amazement, smiling with his typical devilish grin. In his matter-of-fact, deep voice he stated that what we had discovered weren't firebrats; they were maggots. Our amazing find had gone from elation to embarrassment. We were all now trying to back-pedal away from what had moments ago been the source of great pride, and deposit our insects in the nearest trash can.

~∞∞~

VERTEBRATE TAXONOMY

VERTEBRATE TAXONOMY (IDENTIFYING ANIMALS) was offered only during the summer. Thankfully I was able to arrange my work schedule so that I could take the course. Collecting and identifying animals was the thrust of the course. We were encouraged to bring vertebrate specimens — and especially those still living — to class. The classroom looked like a small zoo. Some animals were caged while others roamed around freely, including an opossum complete with young, assorted snakes and lizards, and a very large turtle. That's only a partial list of the critters having free range. It appeared that if they were supposed to have been caged, they weren't. Aquariums and jars did house some of the smaller vertebrates.

Most of the snakes were to have been contained in cages, but some had escaped. Animals would appear and disappear from under the lab tables, and you were always on the lookout for a snake slithering around your feet. One creature in our menagerie was a wood turtle with very large plates on its shell. The plates came to a point and seemed the perfect location for attaching notes. Small pieces of paper were placed onto the shell and distributed around the classroom by the turtle.

We would go on collecting trips that were nothing more than a group of us climbing into the instructor's car and driving the back roads in search of anything that had a spine. It mattered not if it was dead or alive. On one such trip the instructor stopped the car, walked to the edge of the road, and returned with a black snake. He opened the door, sat down, reached his right arm over the front seatback, and dropped the snake onto the floor. As he started the car and drove off, the snake slithered among our feet in search of an escape. A crowded car with a disturbed snake crawling around isn't a good thing, but we were quickly becoming accustomed to living among the wild — whether stationary or in this case mobile — and were just thankful that the snake wasn't poisonous.

Once Upon the Chesapeake Bay

A REQUIREMENT OF VERTEBRATE TAXONOMY WAS an overnight camping trip to the Chesapeake Bay. At night we pitched tents among the biting flies atop Calvert Cliffs, and during the day we voyaged out onto the bay for a little off-shore collecting of marine vertebrates.

Our vessel was a fourteen-foot, semi-V boat with no motor, no floatation devices, and only a set of oars to be used in a boat having just one working oar lock. Regardless, our motley crew boarded the boat, with Dr. Bell attired in his sport coat despite the occasion itself, not to mention the heat. The boat was so overloaded that even the smallest wave caused it to take on water. We were floating only an inch or two above the surrounding bay.

One student decided it would be safer and faster for him to return to shore by jumping out of the boat and swimming back to land. When he jumped overboard, one side of the boat went under the water. As the water rushed in we all leaned to the opposite side to counter the flow, but our overcompensation resulted in more water rushing in on that side. Thankfully we reached equilibrium, but the added weight of the water made the boat ride even deeper in the bay. Dr. Bell observed these events with calm impartiality, only remarking dryly, "I think he's trying to drown me."

The jettisoned student, unfortunately, faired worse than those who remained aboard the water-logged vessel. He had forgotten to take into consideration the large number of jellyfish present in the salty waters. You couldn't put your hand in the water without touching a few and certainly couldn't avoid them while swimming. When we finally met him ashore, he was covered with red bites that were growing larger by the minute. The first-aid offered was neither cream nor ointment, but was instruction to cover the bites with mud. It was supposed to solve the problem, but it didn't. The bites just got bigger, and the student only got muddier. Who would have thought he'd been better off staying on our sinking ship?

THE HAUNTING OF CALVERT CLIFFS

CALVERT CLIFFS — SITUATED JUST ABOVE THE Chesapeake Bay at the end of a tobacco field — is a very good location to both camp and collect fossils — especially shark teeth. The wave action and natural erosion bring the fossils to the surface. Calvert Cliffs is where we relaxed and recuperated after our off-shore collecting.

While settling into the camping phase of our field trip, we began to take notice of a certain classmate who had arrived for the trip just moments before our departure. He had little equipment and was improperly dressed for the extreme heat. We soon learned this was all due to a very recent run-in with the law. He was released from police custody with no time to spare before the trip commenced.

This ill-prepared young man quickly solved his wardrobe dilemma by modifying his attire with a rather large knife he produced from out of nowhere. He took the knife to his jeans, turning them into raggedy shorts. He removed his shirt and tossed it away. He was sweating and the dirt stuck to him, forming a muddy crust. His hair was 1960s-long and unkempt. His overall appearance is largely to blame for what happened next.

Up the bay from our camp of college students was a camp for Cub Scouts and Boy Scouts. The Cub Scouts would walk the shore past us in their blue uniforms, heads bent downward looking for shark teeth. They were always in small groups, laser-focused on the ground, and totally oblivious to the world around them. Above them, dotting the cliffs, was a network of shallow alcoves created over many years by explorers digging into the cliffs in search of fossils. These recesses were perfectly sized for a person to crouch in, undetectable to anyone on the shore below.

Our edgy latecomer, dressed only in his newly cut-off shorts, decided to make his way up the cliff face to one of the alcoves about fifteen or twenty feet above the shore.

He squatted down in an alcove with his knife in hand, essentially becoming invisible. When he eventually stood and moved forward to the point where he was now visible to anyone below, his appearance coincided precisely with the passing by of a group of young scouts. When they happened to look up from the sand to the cliffs, they saw him and were scared to death. They screamed and ran away, only looking back to see if they were being pursued.

I observed this incident from the shore a short distance away, and completely understood why the scouts were screaming and running. While never intending to scare them — let alone chase them down — our mud-encrusted, knife-wielding classmate looked like a prehistoric caveman who was defending his cave from attack. I had to laugh. You couldn't have scripted a more frightening situation for the scouts, nor a better story for them to take home as a souvenir from their expedition.

PLANT TAXONOMY

P LANT TAXONOMY (IDENTIFYING PLANTS) WAS another required course for biology majors. During the semester we collected and identified any plant we could find. Assembling your collection, pressing, preserving, and identifying each specimen was the goal. A collection wasn't complete until it included plants native to other parts of the state. In the spirit of plant diversity, a field trip was taken across the state each spring to Franklin, West Virginia.

It was almost a necessity to attend the spring trip to collect specimens, or have a very good and reliable friend go on your behalf. We piled into cars and formed a caravan of sorts, snaking our way along the very winding roads of Franklin with Dr. Bell leading the way. With eyes like a hawk, Dr. Bell would spot a plant on the hillside and the procession of cars would come to a stop. Everyone would jump out and follow him. He would either bend down and pluck a plant himself, or just point in a general direction and send us on our way. We quickly learned how to read the subtle cues of his body language. We would pounce on any leafy green object in his immediate vicinity and basically defoliate the hillside. Sometimes he told us to collect a specimen, but more often than not we picked the area bare. Sometimes he would laugh and walk away joking wryly, "Those plants are poisonous."

Our field trip also included a stop at Cranberry Glades. It is one of, if not the most southern bogs in the United

States. It is more typical of what you would expect to find in Canada. The area is basically acres of water covered with a thick layer of entangled plants. The blanket of vegetation is several feet thick and can actually support a human's weight. There are also trees and bushes growing on this floating mass, making it appear much like an overgrown field. There is no indication at all that the terrain is floating on water.

We were permitted full access to the area to explore as we pleased, collecting plants found nowhere else in the state. Our primary goal was to collect carnivorous plants such as pitcher plants and sun dew. We began by walking out onto what looked like a field but then started to bounce up and down. In a short amount of time our footsteps had created an undulating surface where trees and shrubs were moving up and down right along with us. How neat it was. A big problem was that if you stood in one place too long you began to sink — not a rapid sinking — but an inevitable slow downward movement. When your feet disappeared, it was neat. When your knees disappeared, it wasn't quite as neat. When the bog hit your hips you were in trouble. You would now need assistance to be pulled to the surface, mud up to your waist, but proudly clutching your valuable, green, and sometimes carnivorous acquisitions.

—∞∞∞—

The Mummy

WHILE PREPARING FOR A COLLEGE FIELD TRIP, I was asked to go to the attic of the science building and gather some supplies. I had never been up there before and took full advantage of this rare opportunity to explore. The attic contained mostly boxes along with a few cages and nets. While peering into one of the boxes, I was greeted by a mummified face staring back at me. I quickly jumped back, having never expected to see something like this. Upon closer examination I saw that it was an entire human body in the box.

This was something I had to share with others. I hurried out of the building and straight to the Ram's Den to find some classmates with whom to share my eerie discovery. We returned to the science building where we were greeted by a few professors. They said there was no reason to go back up to the attic, as all the supplies had now been loaded. This made no sense and foiled my plan to confirm what I had actually seen.

The issue was only discussed once or twice. I couldn't prove anything, and time passed before I was ever allowed to enter the attic again. On that occasion, with witnesses, we entered the attic to find neither box nor mummy. I didn't know what had happened to it.

This should have been the end of the story, but time has a way of changing things. Some forty years later I had the opportunity to speak to a former professor, Mr. Woodward. I decided to ask him if there had ever been a body in the attic of the science building. He responded "yes," and explained that it had been donated to the college as a teaching aide. How it got there wasn't as important to me as the fact that it *had* been there. I wasn't imagining things, though I may have been one of only a very few students who had ever made its startling acquaintance.

—∞∞—

THE LOTTERY

I N 1969, THE PROCESS OF HOW ONE WAS SELECTED for military service had changed. Up until this time, college students could receive deferments until completing their degrees.

All of this changed with the introduction of a national lottery that began on December 1, 1969. The lottery was for all men born between the years of 1944 and 1950. Slips of paper representing all 366 days of the year were put into plastic capsules. Next they were placed into a shoebox and were mixed. The capsules were then dumped into a large glass jar and drawn out one at a time. The first one drawn contained the birthday of the first cohort to be called for military service. The process continued until all days of the year had been drawn and documented, including the 29th of February.

No one knew how far down this list the government would need to go, but when all was said and done, they would reach number 195. For some unexplainable reason I thought the lottery only pertained to nineteen-year-old men, so I didn't pay too much attention to it. However, upon entering the Ram's Den I found the lottery to be the topic of discussion and quickly learned that I now had number 219. A student with the number 366 was sitting nearby, truly showing no concern.

In the spring of 1969, I received a letter from Uncle Sam to report to a facility and be given a pre-induction physical. I boarded a bus to Fort Holabird, Maryland. Friends and strangers, many from college, joined me. Stripped down to our underwear and carrying our valuables in cloth bags, we followed a prescribed order and were evaluated station by station. There were some rather funny things observed, but the overall mood was quite serious. It appeared to me that you had to be near death to fail the exams, though I have since learned that some people were excused from active duty for what oftentimes proved to be frivolous and correctable conditions.

Several potential inductees did try to pull one over on the examiners. One rather large person had the ability to faint at the sight or mention of blood. There was no shortage of blood in the vicinity, as we had all been asked to give some. After fainting several times, he was taken out of line and his examination was over and he was excused from service. Another person tried to fake being slightly crazy. I knew him well and he might have been so, but he was putting on a real show. He was also taken out of line, but kept overnight for further evaluation. His efforts eventually resulted in success.

At the very end of this evaluation process was a table behind which sat several officials who held your future in their hands. In nothing but a pair of underwear, I took my turn and stood in front of a gentleman who announced, "Congratulations. I'll being seeing you in the future." I never saw him again, but saw lots of people dressed just like him when I arrived for basic training the following year.

I think it is necessary to include something about these experiences, as they were an ever-present force in our lives. Potential military service was now a part of all future plans and goals. The carefree lifestyle of male high school seniors and college students today, didn't exist then. Our joy was tempered by the ever-present knowledge that the draft loomed ahead and you couldn't get away from it. Going to college didn't eliminate the possibility of military service, but only delayed it.

Not too long ago, Mr. Woodward, one of my college professors, discussed a "lottery-related" story with me in much greater detail and with a twist. He recalled eating lunch at a table with me and some other students and couldn't help but notice our concern. I was a senior in college, married, and soon to be a father. Mr. Woodward was born before 1944 and not included in this lottery, but could understand our sense of concern. Being only a few years older than most of us students caused him to have a great deal of empathy for our situation. The impact of our conversations still remains deep in his memory. This one simple lottery affected so many individuals. Plans after graduation would be changed for me and my little family, and life would be very different.

THE POTATO CHIPS

G ULA HAS BEEN A PART OF MY LIFE SINCE 1964.
I have mentioned her throughout this book, but our
story is still being written. I had never before heard of
anyone being called Gula, and I have never met another
Gula since. Gula is the name of a Mesopotamian goddess
of healing, though I believe her mother named her after a
rollerskating champion in the day.

The circumstances that bring people together are varied
and unique. I jokingly tell people that I dated and married
Gula because her family had potato chips. They always had
a big shiny bag of Snyder's potato chips. Being the only
child still at home, she had no competition for the chips.
At my house the contents of the bag would have been
devoured in minutes.

Gula graduated from high school in 1968. Just prior to
graduation I asked her to marry me. She said "yes" and we
agreed to wait until she and I had finished college. Plans
have a way of changing, and we decided to marry in June
1969. It was my senior year and Gula left her college studies
and began working there instead to help support us. I was
working on evenings and weekends and our plan sounded

good. Our families were very supportive, but I sometimes wonder if they ever questioned our decision.

I moved to Martinsburg, which was closer to school and work, and we rented a tiny house. I was now living just ten miles from Hedgesville, but that rather short distance represented a substantial cultural divide and marked a tremendous lifestyle change. No longer could I hunt and fish only minutes from my home. No longer would I know all of my neighbors or be a part of their lives. No longer were our parents in charge of our lives. The safety blanket of living at home was gone.

Beginning married life and setting up housekeeping was quite an experience. It was necessary to purchase all of the staples for our kitchen, including herbs and spices that would last for some time. We went to the grocery store and left with everything we needed. The cost totaled $12.26, which at the time seemed like a ridiculous amount to pay. We were young.

Gula and I thought we had it all figured out. I would graduate in 1970 and begin teaching. I sent out applications, accepted an offer from a school in Pasadena, Maryland, and signed a contract. Gula became pregnant and we were excited about our first child due in August of 1970. One's best plans can suddenly change, however, and the military lottery held in December was about to impact our lives. The numbers being called to service kept getting closer to mine, and it was becoming impossible to separate our family plans from the potential for a visit to Vietnam.

Several of my classmates talked about the Army Reserve unit they had joined. I had not considered it before but decided to explore the option. I spoke with a representative from the unit and he told me there were no openings. He would put my name on a waiting list, but at this time it didn't look promising.

Weeks of uncertainty followed, and it was impossible to make future plans. Gula and I both sensed the gravity of possible changes ahead. Then one day I received a phone call and learned that there was an opening in the Reserve unit. I quickly responded, and after raising my right hand and being sworn in, I was a member of the 351st Ordinance Company. All previous plans were scrapped, including the teaching position for which I had already signed a contract. Upon college graduation I continued to work in retail until I was called for basic training. We were now on a new and different path. It wasn't necessarily bad, but was certainly life changing.

I don't actually believe that potato chips brought Gula and me together. God had that match planned all along. It has been forty-six years since we were married, and our faith remains at the center of our lives. We have shared many adventures and wonderful experiences, and have weathered life's inevitable tragedies. Together the two of us are writing the story of our lives which — by the way — we don't plan on completing anytime soon.

AFTERWORD

IT'S EASY TO LOOK BACK AND REMEMBER THINGS not as they were, but as we would have liked them to be. I never do this because it really isn't necessary. I wouldn't change a thing. My childhood and youth were not perfect, but they were certainly ideal.

No matter where I live, I will always call Hedgesville home, as it is the home of my memories. My mother remained there until her death in 1994. My sister and her husband still live there, and their children are just blocks away from them. My brother and his wife live just outside of town near Back Creek. My wife and I have lived and raised our family just ten miles away in Martinsburg since we married in 1969.

Hedgesville has weathered much change over the years, and not all has been good. Many of the original houses and structures were torn down, and some of those remaining are in disrepair. Long gone is the Pure station, the fire hall, and even the post office. The most notable change is the addition of a stoplight at the intersection of Routes 9 and 901. It was needed to manage the high volume of vehicles passing through Hedgesville to the west and north each day, and I do mean *passing through*.

There are far fewer people living within Hedgesville's town limits today, though the number of people claiming Hedgesville residency has increased due to the residential development taking place within the zip code. In fact, the once discernible gap between Hedgesville's town limits and Martinsburg no longer exists. Pastoral farmlands and orchards have been replaced by housing developments and strip malls. To address the expanding population, a new high school was constructed on the edge of town in the '70s and my original high school became a middle school. An even larger high school was opened several miles north of town in the fall of 2013 to accommodate continued growth.

As I visit Hedgesville now, I still see it as it was in my childhood. I fill in the empty spaces where houses once stood. I see the barns, chicken houses, hog pens, and outhouses that once made up my world. Visions of town folk going about their daily lives and of us kids playing fill my head. I hear their voices and smell the food being prepared in each kitchen. Individuals transplanted to the area have no idea what life in Hedgesville was once like or even how the town used to look. They can only see it as it appears today. No photo can express the simplicity, comfort and protection that was felt by the town residents.

When I began writing my stories I had no idea where they would lead me. Writing is now a regular part of my life. Many more stories fill my head and I am eager to put them onto paper. I am so fortunate that my memories continue to surface and that I can share them. At times I feel a little selfish when I write, as I find myself smiling as I relive many wonderful experiences in my mind. Then I remember that my wife saw only a small portion of these experiences and observations, and my children less still, and I know they will only know what I take the time to recount.

It has been my sincere pleasure to try and share the experiences of my childhood and youth through writing. I hope you, the reader, have been able to escape into the town of Hedgesville and get a glimpse of life as I knew it. I am thankful that my writing has encouraged some of you to begin sharing your stories, fleshing out your family trees, and documenting a small part of history that should never be forgotten. The ending of Walt Whitman's poem "O Me! O Life!" reminds us that, "the powerful play goes on, and you may contribute a verse."

What then, will your verse be?

ACKNOWLEDGEMENTS

MANY THANKS TO MY FAMILY AND FRIENDS FOR all of your support and encouragement as I wrote *Goodbye Mister Fifteen.*

Thanks to my wife, Gula, for your devotion not only to me, but also to my writing. You amaze me with your abilities. You are my guide and compass, and have sacrificed much to allow me to pursue this endeavor.

Thanks to our invaluable proofreaders: Mary Campbell, Scott Elliott, Irene Farwell, and Liz McCarthy.

Thanks to Midas the Cat for participating in the photo shoot for the cover, and to Winchester Avenue School for providing the perfect location.

To my daughter-editor-publisher, Stephanie, my deepest thanks for your tireless efforts to complete this project. Your talents continually impress me, and your ability to transform my ramblings into wonderful text is amazing.

A final thank you to everyone who has enjoyed reading my stories. I am humbled by your interest and support as I have attempted to keep alive a wonderful period of time. As you've likely heard me say, "Everyone has at least one book to write. It's called your life." I encourage you to begin writing yours…

ABOUT THE AUTHOR

ROGER ENGLE SPENT THE FIRST TWENTY-ONE YEARS OF HIS life in the small town of Hedgesville, West Virginia, surrounded by his grandparents, parents, siblings, and a large, extended family. He graduated from Hedgesville High School and went on to receive a Bachelor of Science degree from Shepherd College (now Shepherd University) in nearby Shepherdstown, West Virginia. Mr. Engle taught biology at South Hagerstown High School in Hagerstown, Maryland, for thirty years. While teaching there he completed graduate studies and received an advanced professional certificate from the State of Maryland. He also served in the United States Army Reserve.

Since the release of his first book, Stories from a Small Town: Remembering My Childhood in Hedgesville, West Virginia, Mr. Engle has kept an ambitious lecture schedule. In 2013 his book won both an Independent Publisher Book Awards bronze medal for "Best Non-Fiction Book in the Mid-Atlantic Region" and a Next Generation Indie Book Awards finalist medal for "Best Overall Book Design in the United States." In 2015 he was recognized by the Senate of West Virginia and the House of Delegates of the West Virginia Legislature for the work he has done to promote the town of Hedgesville and the state of West Virginia through his writing.

Mr. Engle has been married to his wife, Gula, for forty-six years and they have two children, six grandchildren, and an ever-increasing number of great-grandchildren. He is active in his hometown of Martinsburg, West Virginia, volunteering and serving on various boards and committees. He spends his leisure time enjoying his family, gardening, traveling, eating lots of barbecue as a certified master judge of the Kansas City Barbeque Society, and, of course, writing.